INFLATION

◆

INFLATION

Roots of Evil

◆

Lawrance George Lux

Writers Club Press
San Jose New York Lincoln Shanghai

INFLATION
Roots of Evil

Writers Club Press
an imprint of iUniverse, Inc.

For information address:
iUniverse, Inc.
5220 S. 16th St., Suite 200
Lincoln, NE 68512
www.iuniverse.com

All faults remain solely the error of the Author.

ISBN: 0-595-20499-6

Printed in the United States of America

For all who have ever been laid off or downsized.

Study brings Prevention, which allows for Safety.

CONTENTS

◆

FOREWORD

◆

We need to reformulate our basic Economic precepts, else We risk the hazards of the Past. Economic cycles are produced by economic misallocation of resources. Inflation is nothing but the reflection of this resource misuse. The above statement simply means the Economy is producing the wrong product-mix, and Inflation expresses the magnitude of the error. The digression from what should be produced leads to a split between Consumers who can afford the products which are being under-produced, Consumers who can afford the Products being over-produced, and Consumers who fail in one or the other consumption patterns. Recession always entails when over-produced products can find no buyer, with layoffs of Labor coming. Under-produced products do not initially benefit from the curtailment of over-produced products, as Consumers must have the discretionary income with which to purchase.

This Work attempts to explore the genesis of over-production, or economic misallocation of resources in an divergent Product-mix. The Author believes such misallocation always derives from Product or Profits Hoarding. He tries to present the scenarios under which this Process works. He undoubtedly left out a significant number of affective elements which impact the Process; simply due to the largesse of the enterprise. He still feels his thesis to be sound and accurate, and all Inflation derives from Product or Profits Hoarding.

Lawrance George Lux

Preface

———— ◆ ————

The last Ten years of Economic performance have exceeded almost Everyone's expectations. Now We are dipping into a Recession once more. Traditional Economists adhere to the Cyclic nature of Economics. Booms must always be followed by Busts. Their basic contention states every Period of Economic expansion must be followed by a reorganization (i.e., a Downturn to reallocate resources). Supply-side Economists avoid discussion of Cycles, except to advocate Business welfare as means to initiate Boom cycles. Monetarist Economists assert Cycles can be managed by regulation of the flow of Funds. Neither exhibit any great skill at controlling economic conditions. The real Savior of Economic conditions comes from the use of Real Costs Production. The Economy needs only Real Costs Production, which will provide both Investment Capital and Consumers. This Work is predicated on that thesis.

Chapter I:
Definition of Money

◆

No precise definition of Money has ever been given. Everyone knows what Money is in an innate sense; but developing a specific generic for It, proves exceedingly difficult. Any delineation advanced serves some purposes, but falls short of highlighting real other facets of Money. The failure lies not in the incoherence of the Author; simply in the complexity of function which the Term of Money does encompass. Money, in it's essence, containing the universal fulcrum of exchange. An inclusive definition must be so striated, bi-postulates seem to contradict. Somewhere the message always get diffused in the contortion of the language. The definition for Money here serves the needs of this Work; while not claiming any authoritative inference. Money is defined as a Market-generated Accounting System to ascertain the exchange value of products and services.

What does this definition tell Us? It tells Us first Market forces generate the largesse of assignment of value. The Market is composed of Individuals; each of whom possess their own set of desires, wants, and beliefs. Individual purchasing or selling action impact the assignment of value to products and services. Knowing the extremism of Individual preference available in any Population; One could find an Individual willing to pay $ 1 Million for a common, ordinary toothbrush. One could also find a Seller who would not part with a specific Pocket Calculator for less than $ 5 Million. Most would not pay such ridiculous prices! Therefore the Monetary price for a good or service must be construed as the Mean, not the Average, such a product possesses. It is just that amount of Money which the majority of Consumers are willing to pay for such a thing. This is a very important concept, though it seems very simple. All products and services, except for resource materials, consist of component elements which themselves are products and services. The price of these component elements are determined by their utility in generating the final Consumer preference in the greater product.

Resources materials have a Seller demand price generated by the cost of extracting the materials from their natural state, plus the rate of consumption of the estimated ore. This cost is set by the necessary products and services needed for extracting the ore materials. These necessary products and services are priced by the component elements of their construction, and the Consumer preference which can be generated for these goods and services. The discussion thus far clearly presents an image of a vast complexity being generated by nothing other than the Mean Consumer preferences of a large group of Individuals. Thousands of Mean Consumer preference prices determine each and every Market price for a good or service. The role of the Supplier is establishing a minimum floor based on his Costs of provision of the product, and desire to take the highest bid.

Money is first and always an Accounting system. This alone provides immediate need for evaluation and explanation. Everything in Economic society possesses a Market price, or Monetary fee. This includes land, labor, Capital Equipment, Management; but also Consumer products and services, Savings, Credit and Debt, Interest, Stock and Dividends, royalties, and Entertainment. Resource materials are of two types; mined resources are already a product, while unmined resources are a part of the land value. Clarity assures Everything of

Economic use has a Market value–Monetary worth. A simpler explanation could be Anything held by some Party, which could be desired by
another Party for whatever use; has a Monetary value set by Mean
Consumer preferences through the Market system.

An offshoot of this analysis brings the expression of the total Money
supply equaling the total desired products, services, and resource materials existent. The Money Supply equals the size needed to allow all
accounting of Goods and Services at the current Market prices. Prices
are initially set by Land value, Capital Equipment and basic Labor pro-
visions which take resource materials from their unmined state, to a
position of high desirability product. It can be understood that inputs
of priced labor creates greater, or increased Consumer preference for a
product, or further service. This brought up to insist the Money Supply
increases with the infusion of Labor, at a rate greater than the price of
that Labor; said price of Labor a diminishment from the increase in the
Money Supply, otherwise known as Inflation. The Money supply is also
diminished by depreciation; the process were products lose their
Monetary value through use or inactive deterioration. The Money
Supply grows wherever Labor infuses greater desirability to a Product,
minus Labor and Capital's own cost; the Money supply diminishes at
Garbage Dumps and Junkyards, plus the recyclable capacities of such
materials. The success of the Market lies in the fact the Money Supply
ordinarily increases, with Consumer Demand ordinarily increasing at
the same rate as Product Supply; so there is remarked little Price
increase, and no Price inflation.

The expression of Mean Consumer preferences remain wide and var-
ied. There are product prices, service prices, and resource materials
prices. Labor paid for in two main components–wages and salaries;
with offshoots of royalties, service fees, and contractual maintenance
payments (warranties and retainers). Wages are Money payments to
Labor, treating specific time-lengths of Labor as if they were products.
Salaries are a set payment to Labor, for the performance of set duties;

often accompanied with additional financial incentives for lengthy periods of completion within a set work time-frame. Royalties are financial payments to Labor for development of a product, method of production, or form of Entertainment at a set-piece rate of use; do not be confused by the fact that patent and other royalties rights can be held by business, they are indeed set-piece payments for Labor service. Warranties are guarantees to maintain a product or service for a flat fee; integral to the initial price of the product or service, or extended for a flat fee for a specified time. Retainers are fees paid for guarantees of provision of labor services whenever necessary; said labor services specific in kind. The difference in type all designed to meet specific needs of Labor and Purchasers, to allocate financial payments in a manner best serving Consumer preference.

Land receives payment, through Rent, ore recovery options, and farming and ranching. Land receives Rent from usage for housing, business, or pasturage. All land attains this Rent, which for personal homeowners is exacted initially in the purchase price. This Rent is addition to the Money supply, minus the diminishment of the Money Supply through Property taxation. Ore recovery options (the fees paid for the extraction of oil, gas, or base metals ores) are an increase of the Money supply, minus the diminishment of ore, Labor and Capital costs of extracting the ore, and the Property taxes. Farming and Ranching are themselves businesses, whose profits increase the Money supply, minus the Property taxes paid. The essential characteristic of Land is contained in the fact it holds a residual price, in that it is desired by others; possessing thereby a portion of the Money supply. This portion of the Money supply is diminished by Property tax; lack of utilization of the Land with Property tax assessment, means loss of Monetary value prior to Sale.

Business profits contain the functional drive of the economic system. They are defined as the Excess gains of increasing Consumer preference, minus Labor, Rent, Capital Equipment costs, and Property Taxes. They are further reduced by Capital Equipment depreciation. All modern

Business generally operates on borrowed funds; Interest on such funds is considered as a part of Capital equipment costs, and a diminishment of the Money Supply creation by Profits. Businesses which self-finance with their own funds, still account the interest, and it still is a diminishment of the Money supply created by Profits. Labor costs, in this simple Scenario, include resource materials utilized in Production; because such materials are extracted by Labor and Capital resources, and purchased by Consumer preference–in this case, Business needs for operation. This includes Energy costs, purchased by Consumer preference. Management salaries are also diminishment of the Profits; but not of the Money Supply creation.

Interest is the last area of intense concern for Us, for it is basically the cost of the purchase of some element of the Money Supply. Money, or the possession of it, has a value because it can be utilized to purchase Products; Interest is the payment for possession of that value. Business would call this the Capital Aggregation function. Consumers, whether for final consumption, or for engagement in further enhancement of Consumer preference; find purchasable collections of Money necessary to fulfill Consumption desires. The Interest earned is addition to the Money Supply. There is additional increases to Money Supply as well; to the degree added Consumer Demand increases product or services prices, or forestalls a fall in these prices. The provision of this Credit provides greater competition for limited products and services; adding increases to the Money Supply greater than simple Interest alone.

It would be hard to envision the possibility of Growth in the Economy, as We have seen it throughout the last Fifty years; without this provision of Credit. Previous periods of time held high levels of Growth, but not of the magnitude of the last Fifty years. The rationale for the later period Growth rates, comes solely from this provision of Credit. Restrictions of Entrance into Business were cut in half, by the simple provision of Credit. Business was sustained by high Consumer consumption, occasioned by the use of Credit in purchase. A lack of such Credit in both areas would have cut the Growth in half, at a bare minimum. The downside to this Credit extension has been the loss of the Savings ratio of Labor, due to Interest payments replacement of Savings. This Savings loss has been somewhat curtailed by Labor involvement in business, through profit-sharing programs, Mutual Funds, and Tax reductions through Individual Investment Account Tax delays. It nevertheless constitutes a diminishment of Labor Wages and Salaries in the Pricing system, and therefore is a deflationary pressure on Market prices.

The Money Supply contains the seeds for vast confusion; due to the total complexity of the Issue. The Money Supply increases by an increase of Consumer preference. It decreases by product and service depreciation and the placement of Taxes. Taxes, though, stands not as a complete Villain; to the degree Government increases Consumer preference by the creation of Infrastructure or Consumer Demand through transfer payments, It negates the diminishment of the Money Supply. Recycling of waste products reduces the loss of depreciation; but such recycling cannot be conducted unless it is profitable. Extension of Credit vastly increases Consumer Demand; but causes assured increases in the Resource Market through increased production, and producing enhanced profits for resource recovery. This provides an overall increase of prices.

The above description of the Money Supply function may be called the normal pattern of Money Supply creation. The Economic model derived generates a stable Price formation, with average Inflation of 1.3 percent per year; this due to the artificial Consumer demand created by Credit extension. This Economic model shows incredible stability through the entire spectrum of economic events. Inputs of Population increase, acute shortages of specific labor skills, multiplicity of business competition, and the rising resource costs; do not introduce instability to the matrix. Housing shortages, high unemployment rates, increasing energy demands, high levels of layoffs (downsizing), and destruction by

Weather or Catastrophe; all show little impact on the basic Economic model. The model expresses great strength of resistance to disturbance. One singular factor seems to create great imbalance in the Economic model; advent of Inflation rates higher than 1.3 percent. All of the above-mentioned adverse events, simply transfers Profit ratios to different sectors of the Economy, than were originally placed. Enhanced Inflation, though, quickly creates imbalances in the resource-allocation function of the Market.

Movement towards examination of Inflation brings a wealth of discussion of the Issue in Paper and Classroom, with very little hard definition and data. The first criteria for any problem solution insists on precise definition. One hears lots of talk about the Money Supply, about the printing of Currency, about the effect of Demand deposits, further mention of the expansion of Credit, and even such diverse events as the Rate of Depreciation. A simpler, exact definition often used: Inflation means the increase of overall prices of products from one defined period of time to another defined period of time. This is Inflation? All of the above references explain, or attempt to explain, the cause of Inflation. This definition of causes are flawed, because they literally put the Cart before the Horse.

Return to the above statements finds an incoherent expression stating Inflation to consist of an increase of the Money Supply. The reality remains the Money Supply may, or may not, illicit Inflation. The Money Supply actually holds only direct correlation to the number of Consumers and Suppliers in the Market. Their increase leads to a natural increase in the Money Supply. Inflation is introduced only if Production does not keep pace with the increase of Consumers. The increase in the Instruments which generate the Money Supply, only reflect the increasing complexity of the Market. Complexity brings the increase of diversity of products, and the diversity of resource uses for added products. This Complexity brings alteration of business practice; almost all products Today need to be paid up front, the process of end-of-the-month billing too confusing. Credit instruments like 'running lines of Credit' and 'purchase PRAVDA' (acronym Purchase Average Daily Amounts) brings the businessman ability to move in the Market. The Money Supply tied to the numbers of Elements in the Market with their Credit instruments; examination leads to possible failures of Production to keep pace with the increase of Consumption elements in the Market. (Remember increased Resource Costs are considered disposed with the 1.3% annual Inflation rate of the Normal Model)

It is exactly these failures of Production to keep pace with the increase of Consumption elements in the Market, which is the cause of Inflation. The increased number of Consumers and their desire for a specific Good brings heightened competition for that Good, in the form of higher bids for the Good in Monetary terms. Suppliers of that Good sell to the highest bidder, in the absence of pre-signed production contracts. Inflation consists of the exact differential between original price, and the bid price; the direct result of Production failing production increases to match new entrants into the Consumption Market. (Bid price—[original price + 1.3%OP])

Many would attest Inflation becomes a natural phenomenon, as there does not exist a limitation of the extension of Credit. This is a false statement; Production levels controls the largesse of the extension of Credit, if the normal rules of Credit extension are utilized. Credit extension requires an initial source of funding. This source, under normal circumstances, derives from the profits of Production. Maintenance of standard financial reserves throughout the financial structure constitutes an Inflation generation of 1.3% annually; Our normal Economic model. This guarantees Production increase will grow in relative direct proportion to the Consumer increases in the Market. The 1.3% increase in prices per year reflects the lag-time of Production behind Consumer demand (including resource acquisition increase); effectively Sixty days. Failure to maintain standard financial reserves in Credit extension will generate more excessive Inflation, through mis-allocation of resources; also destabilizing the financial institutions. There also incurs excessive increases to the Money Supply, through above-normal payment of Interest. Credit Extension corruption holds much danger in expansion of Inflation.

Full-circle and still no deep understanding of the source of excessive Inflation; the Search must be extended to the canopy of Inflationary causes. Most Traditional Economists assert there are five: Loss of Resource or Production Capital equipment; Loss of Transport Capital equipment; Mis-Allocation of Economic Resources through Government mal-regulation, or Product or Profits Hoarding; War and it's production for purposes other than Consumption; and Natural disasters and catastrophe which destroy food supplies and grown resources. Each of these stipulated Causes will have a following Chapter devoted to their description. It is sufficient here to simply state these are the sole causes of Inflation; the Money Supply being totally irrelevant, unless affected by One of the above Causation.

Old Economics flat stated Inflation was the result of Governments printing too much Money; a Thesis still continually advanced by non-economically trained Individuals. The printing of Currency falls under the heading of Government mal-regulation, inside Mis-Allocation of Resources. It remains a factor which can lead to Hyper-Inflation, as seen in many Nations; but actually holds slight impact in the Modern Economic World. Financial institutions forestall excess printing of Currency by Governments, because of the loss of validity of their deposits. Such instances of excess printing of Currency come only after Hyper-Inflation is already raging, and Government cannot collect Tax receipts fast enough. Another case of a result being claimed as a Cause.

Currency makes up only about Seven percent of the total Money Supply of a Modern economy. It remains a fairly constant percentage, except in the presence of excessive Inflation. There are increases in the issuance of Currency, while usually matches Population increases; there is a specific amount of transaction in the Economy, about Eight percent, which could not easily be conducted otherwise. This includes Restaurant purchases of beverages and meals, the consumption of Alcohol, purchase of small items from Venders, and Entertainment like Movie houses, Sporting events, Gambling, and Concerts. The growth of Currency must match the needs of Consumers seeking such goods and services; it is indicative this form of the Money Supply has the highest rate of transference. Currency, therefore, grows to fulfill the transaction needs of an increasing Consumer population.

A further point to reiterate must be the continuing acceleration of Monetary transaction. Demand deposit checks have fallen into disfavor, as have Traveler's Checks, etc. There is the criminal potential in such transaction, where funds may not actually be forwarded as claimed. The handling of these transactions are disliked by businessmen for this reason. Further dislike for such transactions reside in the lack of speed in the transference. Such Instruments have to physically travel back to it's issuance source to be validated; only after which will the funds be forwarded. The process can take up to five business days to complete, and deposit of usable funds into business accounts may take even longer. The Depositor Recipient of these Instruments gets no interest on such deposits for the period of physical transference; and is unable to expand his own purchases during this time, using these funds. This constitutes a loss of Production and Consumption potential. Such Instruments are rightfully falling into disfavor.

We live in an increasingly Plastic Card driven World. Electronic transactions of Money hold immense advantages for both Consumer and Supplier. The Supplier receives relief from Criminal activity, knowing positively funding is available. The transfer is immediate, and he can start utilizing the received funds with minimal delay. The Consumer can use such Cards to define what residual funds are left to use, from almost any ATM. Minimization of the use of Checks eliminates the boring process of balancing a Checkbook, what with the necessary tracking of every Check written. Receipts can be retrieved at Source, then plugged into a Expenses software program if Consumer possesses a Personal Computer; allowing even the receipts to be discarded after such action. Real time knowledge of existing discretionary funds, allows for refined Consumption patterns.

ATM and software programming will become even more sophisticated in the near Future. Soon retailers will not offer a written receipt; an electronic receipt will be sent to the purchaser's financial institution, who will send a monthly photocopy of such receipts along with the bank statement. Consumers will have online access to check the proper prices of all items purchased, and retailers will provide online refund upon dispute. ATMs will also evolve; providing seats and cover like certain Game machines at Arcades. A design previewed had four seats, each with a full Computer screen plus keyboard, still accessed by Card, and with central servicing. Any and all financial transactions and detailing could be done from this Center, as well as receiving Currency. This ATM design was for a all-weather unit which was heated for placement on the Street.

Business practice will change as much as Consumer behavior. Display shelves will disappear, replacement being Computer screen; automated Inventory placement taking less space than display floor, while cheaper and less Stocking brings lower Overhead costs. Stores taking only Plastic and returning no Currency, will appear within five years. Consumers will purchase as they would online, though they will not have to type in their Card number; replacing Check-out lines and Cashiers. Personal Computers will have provision to run Credit Cards through an Identifier within five years; turning them into modified ATMs without Currency return capacity. They will have the ability to automatically purchase online, and record the transaction with your financial institution. Purchasing at home will be much like purchasing in Stores through use of demonstration videos online; vastly increasing the business of online sellers, and reducing the Overhead costs of Retailers.

Real Time will become the watchword for the Money of the Future. Time clocks will be replaced by Card insertion in the machine at which a Worker works. A record of the Work done will be kept; pay will enter the Employee's account immediately, at a defined time period; usually one hour. Tax software at the Employee's bank will automatically deduct his hourly tax, based on his previous year's predicted income level. Businesses' operating fund accounts will be debited hourly, at the listed rates–with Overtime pay where necessary. Employees can order Lunch at their preferred Restaurant online and pay for the meal; assured that the Meal and seating capacity will be available upon their arrival. They will be able to order their groceries, or evening Meal, online; assured it will be delivered to their home, at the designated time. Everything will be geared to provision of service, to minimize all delays of productive time.

Robbery will become a difficult task, as Plastic Cards take over the World. A doorway ATM will record your entrance to a Nightspot, giving requested Cash, and assuring You are the Legal Age for the Establishment. You go for a meal at a Restaurant; your waitress hands you a differentiated cell-phone to slide your Card into; the receipt electronically recorded and returned with your bank statement. Police stopping You for a traffic violation will not ask for your license; but for your Charge-Card; your license number will be on file on your Account, and automatically recorded for the Police Report. The Officer will ask if You wish to contest the ticket; if You do not, your Account will be automatically debited for the Fine.

The nature of Money will alter in the Future, to reflect Concerns for Individual Responsibility. Garnishments will become the wave! Laws will be passed; stating underage dependents have rights to Parental wages, probably around a Seven percent garnishment, which will be removed from the Parent's account to the Child's account. The Child will not be able to use the Card, above a set weekly limit, without the Parent's consent; but Big Brother will assure said funds are spent on the Child's welfare. Landlords will also come to insist on a garnishment per hour worked; to prevent loss of Rent. Divorce settlements do no even have to be mentioned. The extension of Credit will flee the Retailers once more; returning to the primary financial institution of the Individual, always assuring garnishment second only to Taxes. Police will be able to trace Criminal activity, by contrasting expenditure records against Employment records. Money will become a fundamental trap, as well as a Medium of exchange, in the near Future.

Money has been defined as it was, what it is Now, and what it is destined to become. The threats to Human liberty are not yet understood, or are the advantages. The centralization of information on the Individual will provide strong support curbing the excesses, which lead to Bankruptcy. Lifetime aggregation of Individual capital will increase, through automatic assistance with professional help. The long-run projection judges the Worker much higher paid, as Management cannot hide the efforts of Labor in the Production process; profit-sharing and higher wages a certainty. Effective Government regulation through Tax Code will eliminate Management malfeasance, and Real Time information will forestall product shortage and inflationary pricing. The control of the Money will bring all changes; information gathering will assure, in Real Time, such control of Money will be advantageous.

Chapter II: Loss of Resource or Production Capital Equipment

◆

The explanation of Loss of Resource or Production Capital Equipment stands as an easy task; simply the loss of the equipment which Producers and Resources Providers use to produce the products which they sell. This loss can be accomplished by Warfare, natural disaster such as Fire, Hurricane, Tornado, Earthquake, Flood, Malignant Damage done by Strikers or Terrorists, and possible loss of Energy sources. Such losses generally have little impact upon overall pricing, unless the losses are widespread in one specific Production sector. Examples can be the loss of the only Diamond mine of an African Nation; a realistic example for the United States would be an Earthquake in the Black Hills which destroyed the Concrete production of the region, a loss of Seventy percent of the output of the American economy. A heavy Earthquake in the Silicon Valley has the potential for changing the pricing structure of the Tech industry. A Hurricane hitting New Orleans dead on, and traveling up the Mississippi River; could potentially cripple the Chemical industry for a significant period of time. A Drought in the American Midwest of the same length and duration as the One which Lewis and Clark traveled through, could bring a quadrupling of Food prices. Floods along the Mississippi and Missouri River basins have been known in Our lifetime, to have taken 8% of the Agricultural land out of production for a year. These are all economic climaxes, which would and do cost American Consumers in terms of lost Income and higher prices.

The exact impact on a Economy and how this impact operates; is one of the great difficulties of Economics. The lost Income of those involved in disturbed production industries is a total loss until production is restored. The issuance of Insurance claim payments and Government transfer payments make up the shortage for the Individuals concerned; but represent a massive increase in Product price to the Economy. The Government and all Insured of the Insurers of the Individuals must refund the Cost of the initial Capitalization to the Individuals; Governments do so by higher taxes, Insurers by higher premiums for Insurance. The Capital equipment has to be replaced, and at the cost price of such equipment at current Market value. The whole of the lost Production during the Period must be considered as an Inflationary price reflecting added Consumer demand in the Capital Equipment Market; a must cost of Capital equipment replacement and transfer support payments to the Individuals imply added Consumer Demand without Production for the Consumption Market.

The impact on the overall Market is an additional cost. Examination of the Consumption Market will first be examined. The loss of Production represents a loss of supply to the Market. The prices of such Products will increase without a loss of Consumer demand. Divergence must be made to description of Complimentary and Competitive goods. Complimentary goods are such goods whose purchase increases, if other specific Products are purchased. Competitive goods are such goods which are bought as a replacement of another Product. The loss of Production will illicit a decline in the purchase of Complimentary goods, and an increase in the purchase of Competitive goods. It is from

this understanding We can determine firmer parameters for disturbance of prices, by losses of such Production.

The loss of Production from such a disaster will generate higher
Consumer demand, and therefore higher prices, for the remaining
Product; if there is no decrease of initial Consumer demand.
Competitive goods will also face increased Consumer demand and
higher pricing; because of their ability to serve as substitute goods for
the lost Production. Complimentary good will face a lessened
Consumer demand, and therefore a lower price schedule; unless they
can serve as a Complimentary good for a Competitive good as well as
for the loss Product. One would expect this would be the total of the
Impact of lost Production, and One would be wrong!

The stable Economic model mentioned above influences the
Productive capacity of Competitive goods in the Economy. Competitive
goods have the ability to substitute for a Product; this though, remains
only a Item substitution, and not an Economic substitution.
Competitive goods suffer Production limitations: lack of resource
materials, higher costs of Production, limitation of physical output, and
constraint of existent Capital equipment. The Economic model outlined above is the most accurate reflection of the actual functioning of
the Economy; it expresses a Marginal dollar utility for previous Capital
investments in all industries. This Marginal utility of Investment
Capitalization assured each Product a specific level of Production of the
Product. Higher levels of productive capacity insist on prior investment
in Capital equipment assets. No Competitive Good can substitute for
any Product more than a range of 14-31% of the Product supply, without further Capital investment in the face of prior marginal utility of
Capital equipment investment in the Competitive Good. This entails a
loss of supply of any Good of approximately Seventy percent, under a
total loss of Production of a Good. A normal Economic model will only
achieve a thirty percent Production of Product with it's Competitive
goods, until recapitalization in either the Product or Competitive goods

production. A stable Consumer Demand will be bidding for a third of the Production and whatever Inventory of the Product had survived the disaster.

The position of Complimentary Goods suffer in both the short-term, and overall. The loss of Consumer demand for their Product means a lower price for Complimentary Goods. This means fore-shortened Profits ratios for their Producers; and less marginal utility investment in the industry. It produces lessened Consumer Demand in the Overall Market; but only about a Three percent reduction of the Consumer Demand increase in the Lost Product Market. It does not significantly diminish Consumer demand; not even close to the same scale of increase of Consumer Demand through the initial loss of Production. One would say it is therefore dismissible; but such Event had cut the marginal utility of investment in the Complimentary Good Industry. This cut of investment might not truly exist in real terms; but it curtails Profitability for the Complimentary Goods industry, making further recapitalization less attractive in both financial and capital equipment depreciation terms. It does this by increasing the Cost of Complimentary Goods production through less productive capital equipment.

Adherence to the Economic model would indicate that the long-run Costs of such a Loss of Production natural disaster doubled the cost of production to the total Market, raise the price of Product Goods and Competitive Goods by 40-88% until recapitalization allows for Productive levels of Product or Competitive Goods to rise to previous Standard, produce an Eleven percent loss of Product market to Competitive goods, and cause a Seven percent under-capitalization of Complimentary Good due to Period loss of price levels. An Economic advantage is gained by the Product industry over the Competitive goods, if the recapitalization was accomplished solely by Insurance payments and Government transfers. The Product industry has new Capital equip-ment without depreciation effects of previous production; while the

Competitive industry has endured the enhanced depreciation effects of extensive full production. The Product industry gets to enjoy the price-lag drop to normalized Production pricing, while the Competitive Goods industry must heavily recapitalize in the face of declining prices. Traditional observance of such Events find there is a long-run Three percent increase of Product prices, above the model's normal 1.3% Inflation rate. This reflects Industry-wide loss of Production for the Period. Normal price structuring, in relation to the rest of the Market, should be expected to come in-line after Twelve years; the normal period for Business Capital equipment depreciation.

The Issue of Insurance claims paid and Government transfer payments need be examined. They are paid for by increased Insurance premium levels on all Insured, and by higher or diverted taxes on Taxpayers. An apparent reduction of Consumer demand; but it is only a surface appearance. The reality consists of a transference from a limited Sector which could not get the largesse of Credit extension; to a much larger Sector whose Individual elements can get the extended Credit for the dispersed amount. This larger element borrows to pay for the loss They endure, but additionally to pay for the increased prices in the Market. This places additional Consumer Demand on the Sector of Production loss, and further increases the Price levels. This makes the Product loss harder to endure because of price competition based upon spread extended Credit. It also reduces the profitability of the Production throughout the Market, based upon the extended Credit, and using the inflated prices of the Sector of Production loss.

Governmental transfer payments are especially poor in eliciting this effect; and maintain inflated prices in the Sector an estimated three percent longer because of lengthened recapitalization schedules, through less impulse to return to immediate production. The extension of Credit itself to the overall Market raises the inflated prices in the affected Sector by an estimated 28% above normal competition, and lengthens the time of heightened competition by Sixty percent. The inflated prices in the Sector generate higher Profits than would generate under normal production. The higher Profits incite higher recapitalization than normal, because of belief in a higher rate of return. It brings an additional push for Capital equipment; inflating the price scales by some Two percent.

The Net results of such Natural losses of Production show the inflationary stresses on the Market. The Product Sector is over-capitalized in terms of Market marginal utility of investment. The Capital equipment is purchased at Two percent more than normal competitive pricing, because of the extensions of Credit through Insurance Claims and Government transfer payments. Competitive goods are also over-capitalized in terms of marginal utility of investment; at the inflated Capital equipment prices. Both Product and Competitive Goods will express less Profitability of Production throughout the Period of Depreciation, because of the over-capitalization at inflated Capital Equipment pricing. Complimentary goods will have been less capitalized than marginal utility investment would dictate, because of loss of Sales during the Period of Loss of Production. This will reflect inflated pricing of Complimentary goods when Production levels return, until the Complimentary goods industry can be properly capitalized.

Examination of the Market as a Whole must be undertaken. Another Economic term is Component Product; defined as a necessary component to the Production of further products. The Production loss being a Component Product to One or more Sector products or industries; there is an escalating Inflation throughout the Market. Needs of Production of Canopy products will increase the Competition for the lessened Product and Competitive goods, by a average range of 20-63% of price increase, than if it is not a Component Product. It will also lengthen the Period of these inflated prices from One-quarter of the depreciation time, to One-third of the Depreciation time, after a return to full Production. Canopy Product prices (Products made from the lessened quantity of Product) will throughout the Period of inflated prices for the lost Product, increase in inflated price by 12-47% of the Price increase of the lost Production component product. Third Generation Production utilizing these Canopy Products, will have a inflated price increase of approximately Two percent.

A Lost Production Product, if not a Component Product, will have inflated prices throughout the Period of return to Production based upon their utility to the Consumer. This becomes reference to Marginal Dollar utility analysis of Consumer purchase prices. Heavy utility components, like Food or Energy, can bring inflated price levels up to 1200-1500% of normal price levels of production. Lesser level utilities like Clothing, Transportation, Water, and Lighting will bring increases of up to 400-700%. Deferrable Goods, likes Cars, Refrigerators, writing materials, and Entertainment will have increases of 70-200%; though pricing in Second-hand markets will triple during the Period.

Overall impact on the Market for such Product loss depends upon the expansion throughout the Market, in terms of Consumption or Canopy Products. Affected inflationary prices will be exhibited in all areas where Consumption or Canopy Products are traditionally used. All the extended area will express inflationary pricing, decreasing pre-dictably by Generation of Production from the Source. The areas reached by Competitive goods will also reflect this same inflationary pricing throughout the total range. Complimentary goods will suffer in the short-term, and in the long-run; to the degree they are tied to the lost Production, or Competitive goods of it. Mandatory Complimentary Goods are devastated by the total loss, Seventy percent of which cannot be made up by Competitive goods.

Chapter III: Loss of Transport Capital

◆

Loss of Transport Capital, in the economic sense, leads to an immense confusion; due to the computation of the elements of Transport Capital. Only an Economist could fully understand the reasoning. The easiest example would be the cost of Fuel: Economics sees a doubling of the price of Fuel, as a halving of the Capital Fuel; because only half of the Fuel can be obtained with the same Funds. So Fuel is considered as a Product for purposes of the estimate of Inflation; but viewed as Capital equipment for determination of Capital assets. Other distracting elements in Economic analysis of Transport Capital could be the average Grade incline of Roads, average per pound pressure of Wind exerted against Transport tonnage, and the straight line delivery average of the Road system to final destination. Economists, like Everyone else, possess their own share of Idiocy, and concentration on minutia. The trouble here, though, is all this detail fundamentally alters the Ton-mile cost of Transport–often greatly. We luckily do not have to delve deeply into this Realm for Our discussion.

Transport Inflation comes from a Wealth of factors, due to the multiplicity of Units, and the Totality moved. Transport costs are also seasonal, due to Weather conditions of Winter, and to the increase in Road Construction during the Summer. Road Construction can delay and slow to the point of costing almost another mile per diesel gallon, said Fuel cost needed to be computed into the overall analysis. The loss of Transport Capital and loads must be computed, from the source of Road accident; this must be separated into Human Error and Crosswinds. Railroads have the problem of hitting Cars and Trucks because of Driver carelessness; something which causes delays in Transport miles covered. The above, due to the loss of Transport Capital and delays, raise the Ton-mile cost by an average $.02 per mile.

Bad flying weather can cause up to Seven percent of Cargo flights to be canceled. The Cargo is finally delivered, but the down time is considered loss, because other tonnage contracts could not be delivered. Government regulations, limiting the time Truckers can drive to 10 hours before a break, leads to a average down-time of Capital use of Six hours per day. Self-owned Trucks have an average of 3.5 days downtime per Week. FAA regulations are in-process to limit in-line Pilot and aircrew service to 14 hours per day. This is estimated to mean the hiring of Nine percent more Pilots, at an average salary of $64,000 apiece per year. Transport economic analysis hold complexities not imagined by the layman.

We must finally turn to an analysis of Transport, and it's effect on the total Economy. A fundamental element of Transport impact, is a practice of Economic analysis called Final Placement. Economies grow from more pastoral settings, to the complexities of high technological Sectors using economies of placement Production. Placement Production concerns the greatest marginal dollar physical locale to produce; computing things like wage scales of the area, proximity to necessary resources or Component products, proximity to cheap Energy, cheap land and Plant capitalization, and ease of Transport of Product. Placement Production provides for cheaper Production, but places greater pressure on Transport. Final Placement of Product of WWI industry, when considering all Products produced, was about 37 miles from Production site. Final Placement of Product for the present Economy remained highly debated, from 560 miles as a minimum, to 1708 at a maximum. (Note of Author: Commentary has already disclosed a doubt of the expressed figures. I explained Final Destination Product was a ratio. The milage of all Component parts and the miles they traveled had to be scaled for bulk, to arrive at a Standard Transport Mile [STM]. This is done by dividing the total part components per transport Unit by the milage delivered.) The great discrepancy between the two figures comes on Economist individual desire to include Component Part Production in the computations; Some find the transfer of raw resource unacceptable for inclusion, Others will not account the component parts travel of listed Component Parts. We are talking about individual Product-miles of Transport, in either case; from origin of production to Consumer.

Study of Placement Production provides Insight into the problem. Placement generally provides great advantage to the area picked; in terms of new jobs at some marginally higher rate of pay, increase in the property tax base, greater Profits for Retailers in the area, etc. It also has a downside in Economics; the area picked generally has to improve the road system to the Production, to provide Transport access, as well as Worker access. This generally means an average of 31 percent increase in the immediate area of Twelve miles, and a Seven percent increase in the surrounding area of Fifty miles. Construction of this new road system comes at a price of $27,000 per mile; total milage increase determined by previous road development in the area. The increased Transport and Worker traffic to the area, insists on a percentage increase of Fuel stored in the area; necessary storage determined by number of vehicles, at an average Construction cost of $70 per gallon of storage capacity. This discussed all is an increase of Transport Capital stock, a gain though expensive; the problem comes from the fact Transport Capital stock has a depreciation rate between Four percent and Nine percent, depending on the type of Stock. Economic purposes would dictate that this depreciation is a loss; but Crazy people like Economists insist this is inflationary price increase in the Transport industry.

We return to Final Destination Product ratio, and stipulate that it has been increasing, whatever the real value is; and declare that it is not inflationary price increases in Transport, in and of itself. The increase in miles of the ratio requires an investment in Transport Capital, and in Energy use; to accommodate the further transport of Product a greater distance. This increase in Transport Capital is not inflationary pricing; but increase in Capital Investment. The increased Energy use also is not inflationary, in and of itself. A more specified analysis must be introduced for understanding.

Inflation enters the Final Destination Product ratio when the increased milage requires account for depreciation on Transport vehicles for the added milage, the increased costs of producing the added fuel to travel those miles, and the Wage cost of hiring and training more Transport personnel to maintain Work schedules. Remember the fact Transport personnel hours incurred in delivery of Product is not inflationary, but a simple increase in Productivity. We look for the inflationary price aspect of Final Destination Product ratios increasing. The relative points are the dollar value increases of Depreciation of Transport Capital, the overall rise in the cost of Fuel because of the added Fuel necessary, and the added exhaustion of Labor assets by the added milage which is reflected in higher hiring and training costs. One has to be very careful to separate added Capital stock increments, from inflationary pricing. A maze of Statistics will not help the discussion, so a simple statement will suffice to state: The Final Destination Product ratio increase add approximately $.002 per mile increase in inflationary price. One must honestly state more Economists would disagree with this figure, than would agree.

We finally arrive at a place where We can have some fun; as all of the following are definitely inflationary pressures in the Transport Sector. Tornado, Storm, and Hurricane destroy approximately .0017 of the Fuel Storage capacity of the United States per year. It is only the speeded depreciation on the Capital stock which is inflationary pricing for the

Transport industry. Human Error costs the destruction of approximately $7 Billion of Transport stock; again it only the accelerated depreciation schedule which is inflationary pricing. Almost $3 Billion worth of Cargo loads are destroyed per year from all Causes; the increase in Insurance premiums from the claims paid for such Cargo are the inflationary pricing element. Delays in delivery due to reduced speed of Transport, nothing said of validity of Speed limits and Construction barriers; can be related in terms of added fuel exhausted.

The final real component of inflationary pricing in the Transport industry again concerns Human Error of a different order. An estimated 39% of total Cargo transported in this Country is sent on the wrong form of Transportation. Much of this misallocation comes from bad reputations of certain elements of the Transportation system. The Railway systems have shown terrible resistance to providing reliability of delivery schedules; and they express horrid aptitude for routing correct vehicles to correct site. Dispatchers develop personal relationships with Truckers and Trucking companies, and route to Trucks; simply because it can be hauled in that manner, though a much higher cost. Many Companies ship by Air Transport, though there is no short period delivery constraint. Others use UPS or FedEx, though there is no time element involved, and US Mail would deliver at a quarter of the Cost.

The cheapest form of Transport in the United States consists of Barge traffic on the River system, for both light bulk, and heavy tonnage. Only Three percent of the Ton-mile potential of Barge traffic is utilized, and Barge Transport remain 85% under-capitalized. Barge traffic will save $.03 per Ton-mile over Railroad transport, and $.11 per Ton-mile over Truck transport. The inflationary price of this Transport is the differential of Transport used times the actual Cargo weights hauled, minus the potential cost of Barge Capitalization and depreciation.

The lack of Railway use is actually worse than for Barge transport. Railroads can reach approximately five times the locations as Barge traffic, and has an effective spread pattern equivalent to Trucking. The differential between Railroad and Trucks is approximately $.08 per Ton-mile. Railroads could haul Sixty percent of the Cargo now hauled by Truck. The differential times the total tonnage, minus the necessary Railroad capitalization, plus the reduced Trucking capitalization, would give the inflated Transport pricing.

The usage of UPS and FedEx for deliveries not requiring a 3-day time limit remains a vast under-utilization of the US Mail, and the price differential times total Cargo loads is the inflationary Transport pricing. US Mail capitalization is not mentioned, because the Organization is over-capitalized to the point where it could handle the added traffic without Capital investment. The other Transport companies are over-capitalized as well, without the need for the full range of full Transport services. The depreciation of the over-capitalization plus the exhaustion of Fuel under conditions of partial Cargo load capacity stands as the inflationary pricing of Transport.

The multiple use of Air transport for Cargo with no priority holds the worse excess in the American Transport Sector. Air Transport has a differential of $.58 per Cargo mile with the US Mail; $.77 per Cargo mile for ordinary Truck mass transport. American Transport works with an constricted Air-space scenario, and restriction of Air Cargo transport to priority items, have an estimated reduction of Air traffic of Thirty percent. There could be a further reduction of Air Cargo transport capitalization of Seventy percent. The transfer of Production facilities from Avegas fuels to Gas and Heating fuels, is estimated to save the American Consumer $.11 per gallon; were Air transport reserved for absolute priority shipments. The inflationary price in the current system consists in the differential of transport cost, plus the differential in cost of producing aviation fuel over Diesel. It is noteworthy that Jet airplanes have twenty-eight times the Fuel consumption per hour than Trucks, and actually requires Seven times as much Fuel to move an equivalent amount of Cargo the same distance.

The true normal source of inflationary pricing in the Transport industry comes from the haulage of partial Cargoes. The American Railroad system be the worst violator; having specialized Cargo transport suited for few uses. The method Economics estimates the deadhead miles is similar to the formulation to determine Final Destination Product ratios: Take the total Individual unit tonnage potential, and divide by the number of miles traversed empty. Partial Cargo is determined by $(T/M—[T/M]/2)$, where T=total tonnage capacity, M=milage traversed, and the use of Two as the most likely average of percentage of part loading. It would seem easier to use simply $(½)(T/M)$, but there is the situation where partial Cargo is picked up at a point after the drop of the previous load. Thereafter the Equation becomes $(T/M—[T/m\#/2 + m^*])$, m# equals the hauled partial Cargo miles, and m* equals the miles traveled deadhead. Depreciation per mile traversed must be established and set a value of D. Fuel usage must be determined under full Cargo hauling (F1), and fuel consumption for deadhead empty hauling (F2) must be set. The total Equation becomes quite complex:

(F1) $T/M—[T/\{m\#/F1/2\} + \{m^*F2\}] = NPF$, normal pricing fuel;

(F1)$(T/M)—NPF = IPF$, inflationary pricing fuel;

$D(T/M—[T/M]/2) =$ normal depreciation cost (NDC);

$(D—NDC) + IPF =$ inflationary Transport pricing (ITP)

The numbers are clearly complex, and the Author assuredly is no Mathematician. The Equation also proves to be very incomplete, with no inputs for Labor depreciation and recapitalization increase. It is sufficient for the Reader to recognize approximately 37% of Railroad freight rates are inflationary pricing. This must be remembered in the light that Railway is the third cheapest method of transportation, and can reach almost all sections of the American economy; unlike the cheaper means of Shipping and Barging.

Trucking expresses far less deadheading, but almost the equal in partial Cargoes. The Math is exactly the same as for Railroading, except Labor depreciation has a much higher value in Trucking. It makes up almost Thirty percent of the inflationary pricing of Transport for the system, whereas Labor makes up less than one percent of Railway inflationary pricing. Nothing much need be said further, except to give approximate number; about Nine percent of Trucking freight rates are inflationary pricing. Actual numbers remain hard to tabulate; yet, it is probable Trucking has captured Sixty percent of all freight haulage. One can expect Trucking to supply almost half of the inflationary pricing of Transport.

Normal Transport pricing of Air Cargo stands as a huge cost; the inflationary cost of shipping non-Priority freight Air freight is incredibly high. It probably makes up all of the remaining total remaining inflationary Transport prices, because Railroads provide only about 15%, and Shipping and Barges are negligible (perhaps 3%). Planes lifting off with only partial Cargo, makes huge inflationary pricing inroads in the Transport industry. Estimates exist which states normal Aircraft usage runs only 55% of Cargo capacity. The infrastructure costs of maintaining airports, air traffic control, aircraft maintenance, and ground crews for the airports; insists inflationary pricing would inhabit more than Fifty percent of air freight rates.

The last Item on the agenda must be the area of Passenger traffic. Transport Studies are traditionally divided into Freight and Passenger traffic. This division is basically to ensure the Passenger traffic instabilities of scale, do not ruin the Cost estimates of Freight transport. Simple studies indicate that Flight per Passenger mile costs Six times as much as Passenger Car; Eleven times more than Bus transport; and Twelve times more than Rail transport. Travel by Ship should be cheaper than any form Today; but Cruise line rates compete with Air traffic in expense, both in Individual expense and economically, because of the high living provided.

The real inflationary costs of Passenger traffic are well-hidden from the Consuming Public. The depreciation life of Buses intercity expresses that it hauls less than 18% of the Passenger load capacity possible through it's life. This means 41% of the price of the intercity Bus remains inflationary pricing. It also means that It burns over 68% of the Fuel It consumes needlessly; to a total cost of $14,000 per bus, per lifetime depreciation. Both must be considered inflationary price increases. Cross-country Buses operate at an 87% capacity, up over 30% in two decades, due to shutting down of unprofitable routes and a slimmed-down schedule. This can be considered to reduce depreciation lifetime inflationary price increase to less than $800 per vehicle.

The subject of Passenger cars are generally avoided by most Economists. Almost all vehicles are built with a capacity of four or more. Eighty-two percent of all Passenger car miles are driven with Two or less in the vehicle. This works out economically in a most horrible way! Lifetime vehicle depreciation would claim an inflationary price per vehicle of more than $8700. Inflationary pricing for the consumption of Fuel would list almost $4100 per vehicle per lifetime; and causes a $.47 per gallon increase in Fuel prices in the Country. The inflationary price increase in road construction, which must be based on depreciation and not increased construction, still runs to $217 per vehicle per lifetime. This Author does not criticize, just computes data; he himself, loves the privacy and personal comfort of a personal vehicle.

Chapter IV: The Inflation of War Production

———————— ◆ ————————

The more horrid examples of inflationary Transport prices were left to this Chapter, for Two very real reasons; One, peace-time disruptions are too localized in area, and too quickly rebuilt, to affect Transport pricing drastically, using only accelerated depreciation schedules, and rarely causing less than a percentage point of Inflation in Transport prices. The second primary reason being only Warfare delays repair of Transport facilities for suspended periods of time, while destroying wide segments of the Transport infrastructure. Physical tonnage is actually forestalled, rather than significantly delayed. War and Earthquake alone have the potential for production of Area inflation, due to the lack of supply; even Volcanos do not reach significant distance to disrupt the Supply function.

War Production holds many more sources of Inflation than simple Area Inflation. The entire field of military supply stands as inflationary pressure. This can be said because such production is not for the furtherance of increased production, or for Consumption to raise the Standard of Living for Anyone. It is production of Product for use outside the Economic model, without expectation of return of material resources to the Economic model. It is the permanent deployments of resources beyond the range of material use by the Economy. All

Material resource, Plant, Labor, and Capital used for military supply production, defined in total Costs of Production, computes as total inflationary Production cost; reverberating through the Economic system as increased prices.

The above analysis holds great importance, because of the complexity of the Issue. War is Inflationary; but War Production, defined as the provision of military supples and weaponry, is totally Inflationary, with or without actual warfare. The only recovery from this Inflationary pricing lies in recycling of War Production materials for domestic use. This occurs only about at a rate of Sixteen percent recovery. The important point of this analysis lies in the consideration that the Inflationary pricing is Permanent, because of the exit of material resources from the Economic model or system. The Price structure will not alter to a lower price, until such time as more efficient Recapitalization occurs in the system. This Recapitalization does not replace resource, though, only making more efficient use of remaining resource. Some element of Inflationary price will forever remain in the system, due to the consumption of resource.

Readers may imagine the Author to be some Peace freak, hating the practice of War. This is not the case; being as Patriotic as Any, and more Hawkish than most. The fact remains War Production brings Inflation, without any permanent counter. The price Inflation represents a loss in the Standard of Living for many, or all, in the Economic system. War Production planning need consider long-term rises in Price in the Economy. Failure to do so brings sudden Price Inflation of heavy impact, wildly in some Sectors of the Economy. Evaluation of the long-term decrease in the Standard of Living should also be considered. Military and Politician tend to pursue resource-intensive weapon systems and military supplies, because such enhance their personal image. Less resource-wastage and greater effectiveness can often be found elsewhere.

The above discussion focus on long-term, or Permanent Inflation to the Economy by War Production. Some Economists like to call this type Residual Inflation. It's impact will not appear in magnitude until after a succession of years devoted to War Production. The example of the United States could help explain the process: The United States organized and maintained a structural War Production between 1940 and the Present, of duration of Sixty-One years. The initial five years committed 10-12% of Total Production to War Production, the second five years committed only about 4% of TP to WP. The following 32 years committed 10-12% of TP to WP. The remaining time committed about 6% of TP to WP. The current President indicates He would again raise the commitment of resources to WP to a scale of almost 8% of TP (revised to 9% since the Terrorist Attacks. These are the figures of estimated commitment of resources of Land, Labor, and Capital Equipment to WP, with the addition of raw materials consumed. The total of these materials were extracted from the Production and Consumption Sectors, so it must be considered total inflation. The Author has not did any mathematical calculations on the Subject; but suggests that long-term Residual Inflation through War Production is responsible for Thirty percent of the Inflation increase since 1940.

War Production inflation does not end with long-term Residual Inflation. It's greatest impact lie in the short-term. The reason for this contained in the Priority given to War Production materials. The Government either orders Manufacturers of WP to pay Top Dollar in the bid for materials, or sets restrictions on the production of domestic products. The first leads to an over-capitalization of the Resource recovery Sector, and drives up the price of Competitive Goods of the War Production. Restrictions on the production of domestic products brings Inflation in the Consumption market. How rapidly this occurs will amaze those unused to this data. The average rate of wage per hour in the WP sector in 1940 was $.30. This had risen to $.65 per hour by 1945. Domestic Production wages in 1940 was about $.21 per hour; this had altered to a estimated $.41 per hour by 1945. Many would claim this is an unfair assessment, because of the draft of Labor into the Military; this, though, was a draft of Labor resources for War Production.

Another assessment may prove more enlightening: The cost of a roll of Barbed Wire to farmer and rancher was about $1.25 per roll. Barbed Wire was unavailable in the War years, except for the Black Market. There it was priced in excess of $20 per roll. Restrictions of production were removed after the end of WWII, and returned to full domestic production by 1947. The cost of a roll of Barbed Wire in 1947 was almost $6.70. The returning Military troops were not fully re-integrated into domestic production until mid-1948, yet the cost of Barbed Wire per roll did not decrease. No One will deny Barbed Wire to be a ferrous commodity of high resource wastage, and the rise of Price for it was actually too long delayed; but overall domestic products prices climbed at rapidly as did the wages in the WP sector, while wages in the domestic production Sector dropped somewhat with the return of veterans. The difference of rate increases between domestic production wages and Prices indicate Residual Inflation of War Production.

The period of the Vietnam War is also very illustrative as to the impact of War Production. A Family Man with three dependents could support his Family very easily on $100 per week, in the year 1960. He could do this without his wife working, and might be a Doctor, Lawyer, or Judge. Plant workers cleared some $65-80 a Week in 1960. Many claim the analysis should be started in 1964; but U.S. commitment to ballistic missile development and nuclear submarines started around 1960 at full production. 1973 can be seen as the end of American military supply of the South Vietnamese, though it did not fully end until 1974. A single Plant worker found it hard to support himself alone, if he cleared less than $100 a Week in 1973. Judges averaged around $270 per Week, and both Lawyers and Doctors were averaging considerable more. Most Economists would assert the analysis to be flawed, because of non-inclusion of the Great Society massive welfare spending. This Author maintains that Domestic Production during this Period grew at a superior rate to the price inflation in the domestic market throughout the Period. There should have been no price rises, even with domestic welfare transfers; the minimization of taxes for Corporate business and War Production were the only causes of Inflation in the Period. The Government Debt grew from a 1963 Kennedy proposed $100 Billion to a high (the Author has to really search his memory, which is doubtful) of between $565-840 Billion in 1975.

The National Debt had grown to almost a Trillion dollars by 1980, when Reagan took over as President in 1981. There is no doubt welfare transfer payments(especially Social Security and Medicare) caused a great increase in the Debt. The Author here must contend with claims the Social Security program was solvent throughout it's history. He must counter-assert a process of shifting the real tax impact from general Governmental revenues to Social Security taxes; Individual taxes were reduced in real terms, as Social Security taxes were raised. The real Inflationary push of the Period remained a Corporate welfare program which maintained War Production at high levels throughout the Period, and the administration of Reagan. The National Debt increased every year and rapidly: Kennedy proposed a National Debt of $100 Billion as a high. Richard Nixon was used to a yearly increase of such magnitude, by his leave-taking. Reagan added a Trillion Dollars to the National Debt during his Eight years.

Examination of the entire Period from 1960 to 1989 shows an increase of War Production throughout the Period, not only because of inflated pricing; but an actual product level increase per year. Domestic Production managed to achieve increases on a par with the increase of Inflation, and the increase of Consumer Demand; though it did not maintain this pace consistently, or create the number of jobs necessary for the expanding Economy. This growth of Domestic Production indicates there should have been an Inflation rate no greater than 1.3% per year throughout the Period; short-term anomalies would have reflexed back to the normal Standard in succeeding years.

Many Economists would cite the Energy Crisis as a major cause of the Inflation rate of the Period. This is not wholly accurate; the Energy Crisis was initially caused by Warfare between other Nations than the U.S. This Warfare was brought about by War Production in the United States and it's Competitors, who armed the Participants. The War came to an end, but Oil Companies refused to surrender the huge Profits coming from the inflated prices. They were supported by a U.S. Congress paid well by political campaign contributions from the Oil industry; and who enjoyed the advantages of a major Gas Tax applied in the Gas shortage, and did not want to disturb Voters by raising taxes elsewhere. The Energy Crisis resolved first as a vast increase in Resource recovery Costs, then into a maintained monopoly supported by both Oil industry and Government.

A full examination of the Energy Crisis lies beyond the capacity of this Author; who would need the assets of a Research Foundation to give seminal analysis. It is sufficient to state there was never acute shortage of Energy at any time during the Period. The question was not of sufficient quantity, simply of the Price which had to be paid. Considering the total increases in Energy Cost to the total value of Production during the Period; the Energy Crisis should not have caused greater than a Seven percent Inflation rate through the Period of Resource Recovery recapitalization, or Twelve years. This would indicate a total Inflation of 84%. The extension of Credit throughout the Period should have raised the inflation rate per year for the Twelve years to 8.3%. The commonly-assumed rate which most Economist accept is 9.4%. It is noteworthy War Production during the Period was the lowest physical levels in relation to Total Production levels in these Twelve years, as any years between 1950 and 1992.

War Production has many other impacts on Inflation, all relatively short-term. One aspect is the over-capitalization of the Resource

Recovery Sector, under conditions of sustained War Production. This leads to a diminished Profits picture for the Sector, with a drop of War Production. This leads to a 'Flare' Inflation where the entire Sector raises Prices to maintain Profits. It can be joined by a 'Continued Momentum' Inflation, if the Resource Recovery Sector refuses to lessen it's recapitalization schedule, because of loss of Prestige or Government pressure to keep the Sector viable for War Production. Either of these two types of Inflation can maintain Sector pricing about Three percent over Normal Economic model, for sustained Periods of up to decades. Yearly overall Inflation rates can be increased from 1.3% to 2% per year, from this type of Resource Sector Inflation. The Author perceives it's existence in the American economy Today, and it's presence ever since 1960.

There is a Minimum War Production level which can evolve, and is most definitely present in the American Economy Today. This is not some Evil hidden process; just the reflection of Modern Production, both Consumers and Producers altering business practice to best achieve efficiency. Military staffs are set up, geared to design, inspect through the Production process, test, distribute to active units, and supervise through the Production process. Suppliers expend large quantities in hiring qualified labor, in R&D, in testing, and capitalizing Mass Production. Both groups need a minimum level of supply of these specific products, in order to keep their jobs and maintain Profits for the Industries involved. What is beneficial for the rest of the Economy, is hazardous in the War Production Sector; as it is production for non-Consumption purposes.

There are several remedies which lower the impact of Minimum War Production levels. The greatest is alteration of Military assignment methods. Assignments should be posted as in the Civil Service, with officers and enlisted personnel bidding on them. Security could be maintained by posting only the MOS qualifications necessary, with Bidders supplying a full resume of experience. Military Policy altered to limit any Duty Station Posting to Three years' duration, with no continuous Postings. This has the benefit of spreading technological knowledge and experience to an increasingly qualified Military force. Competition between suppliers can be maintained through insistence on at least two bids for every Contract award; and disallowance of the same Contract being awarded to the same Bidder in successive contract periods. The dislocation to Contract Production schedules could be minimized by Personnel changes which would allow hiring Personnel away from a previous Award holder; and transfer of Research and Production facilities at a Contract pre-set Price, if these facilities were financed by Government funds for Weapons systems. This Practice, while complicated, is enforceable; and estimates indicate a Savings to Government of some Seventeen percent of total War Production contracts.

The major problem of War Production Inflation lies in the fact over half of it's impact is hidden in the greater Economy. Over half of the Military purchases made come in competition with the Private Sector in the Marketplace. This concerns raw resources, Food, Fuel, Clothing, Construction materials, and Vehicles like Trucks and cars. This creates an increased Consumer Demand, without increased numbers of Consumers. This leads to higher Recapitalization funding than would be normal; and all Consumers of Products pay for that added funding. The purchases also represent an overall reduction in Average Standard of Living, because actual Consumers have to pay an increased share of their earnings for the Products they purchased before, because of the increased competition for those Products. This provides for several hidden aspects to War Production Inflation.

Actual Wars generate a vast increase in War Production. There is a vast increase in Consumer Demand at these times, and a large rate of Inflation. The War is concluded by the Victors, and there is a decrease in their War Production. Is there an immediate fall in Prices to reflect the reduction of War Production? The answer is Yes; but the drop never represents a quarter of the normal response drop. There remains the fulfillment of Military contracts left over; the fact of raised Resource Recovery capitalization; the changeover period to transfer to domestic production; and long-term reduction of Wages of those engaged in the War Production. All of the above push towards maintenance of the inflationary prices of the War effort.

Business enterprise are loathe to lower prices, as they desire to maintain the Profit ratios of the War effort. They are assisted in this effort by returning Military personnel, who use their back pay to re-enter the domestic market. Consumers have become accustomed to the higher prices of the War effort, and have scheduled such prices into their Consumption budgets; expressing a willingness to compete on a higher Price level, even though this is a lowering of their Standard of Living. The history of the United States Economy indicate that the temporary War inflation of World War II, with the injection of the Korean Conflict; did not dissipate until almost 1960. The temporary War inflation of the Vietnam War did not dissipate until after 1992.

The Residual, or Permanent Inflation of War Production always remains in force throughout the Period of Depreciation of all Capital Equipment purchased under conditions of War Production inflation. Then it reduces only to the point of lessened resources to supply Domestic Production. Other aspects of this Permanent Inflation is increased Governmental staffs, both Civil Service and Military. It is indicative that it took a change from Democratic to Republican administration, to get rid of the War Industries Board of World War I; this change occurred in 1923.

We have, Today, a Veterans Administration which handles a third of the Veterans as was handled in 1960; with a staff more than doubled, and a budget of 3.5 times that of 1960 even when adjusted for Inflation. Military Relocations staff handle only Three percent of the yearly transfers they handled in any of the World War II years; they do so on a budget some 17.5 times that of their World War II counterparts, even after adjustment for Inflation. An estimated Twenty thousand Military officers, enlisted personnel, and Civil Service personnel handled the complete routing of Twelve Millions American Servicemen in World War II. They did this without Computers, from dozens of warrens in Washington D.C., all built at the turn of the Century. It is estimated that the $7 Billion Dollar Pentagon requires $170 Million a year to operate, with over 135,000 assigned Military personnel and Civil Service employees; They somewhat ineffectually route some 970,000 Military personnel. This is very definitely hidden Inflation.

The final comment on the hidden nature of War Production Inflation contains the thought War Production, after it's first years' impact; remains totally hidden as long as War Production growth does not exceed the total growth of Production. The Inflation of pricing is still present; but ignored because of growth of TP. Additions of Consumers to the Market, together with their lines of Credit, are considered the sole culprits of the witnessed Inflation. No One mentions that 83% of all War Production could be directly transferred to Domestic Production, with a direct changeover Period of less than a Year. This translates into an annual Growth rate in Standard of Living equal to WP(.83).

Chapter V: Natural Disasters and Resources Shortages

◆

Natural disasters remain a potent source of Inflation in the Modern World; though Economic reaction be swift. The average closure of a Railroad line is a matter of Days, rather than months of old; actuarial statistics maintain Inventories of rolling stock, track-laying equipment, and rails in repair depots placed to respond quickly anywhere in their Sector. Highway crews react even faster; almost always having Incident breaks of Roadways resurfaced within a Week. Rare is the modern Airport who closes longer than Twelve hours, even under blizzard conditions. These, though, are all Incident closures which do not affect a large section of the Transportation system; costing little Inflation other than the hastened rate of depreciation.

The impact of Natural Disasters over large areas, though, can be incredibly devastating. Every time a Hurricane hits a section of American Coast, One hears a claims of Hundreds of Millions or Billion of Dollar loss. Most of these claims come from the increasing population densities of these areas. No Economic Study to reach the Author's knowledge, has ever been modeled to determine Average Capital Loss, by the intersection of Population density per scale mile and Wind speed. This would have to be supplemented by Wave surge per density square mile affected. It must be remembered most Hurricane damage consists of Residential property damage; not a loss of Productive Capital, unless Labor resources are lost. Recapitalization of this Residential property is inflationary, if Depreciation rates are again higher than average National rates of Residential Property depreciation rates.

The Productive Capital lost to Hurricanes consist mainly of shipping, Port facilities, Retail businesses, and Fishing and Shipping industries. Some additional area of Agricultural land loses Production for a year. The latter eventuality comes from the Storm line which precedes the Hurricane, and travels through the Country, until the force of the Hurricane is dissipated. Actual statistics are not available to the Author, who loosely estimates the minimal level Hurricane will drop a minimum of 2', or twenty-four inches of Rain, between the Coast and the dissipation of the Storm line. He estimates that every upgrade of Hurricane level will dump an additional twenty-four inches of Rain on the Area. This often occasions Flood conditions in the areas affected. Flood conditions, depending on Flood levels, will destroy some percentage up to 100% of the Agricultural productivity for the Year, or the following Year, if the drying process is delayed. Flood can destroy up to almost Four percent of the Transport vehicles in the Area; possibly destroy 5-7% of the Bridges; possible washout sufficient Roadway and Railway to close the road systems for a lengthy period of Time. Production may be interrupted in the Area for up to a Month's duration; due to the inability to get raw materials, inability to ship Product, or absent Labor resources who are cleaning up residences.

The inflationary price increase of such Conditions consist of the speeded depreciation schedules of lost Capital, residential and Productive. The losses of Production Time result in a drop of Production inside an increased Consumer Demand, to which has been added a desire to recapitalize lost facilities. Little statistical study has been made by the Author, who can only estimate that Hurricane damage accounts for a Two percent yearly loss of Production in the areas affected; averaged through all the areas affected in the United States through it's productive history. Recapitalization of lost facilities remains much higher, with an estimate of Capital destruction at half the normal rate of Depreciation. A accurate assessment that 3% of U.S. territory affected in any given Year, leads to prediction of a 0.02 to 1.7% inflationary price rise overall because of Hurricanes. Withdrawal from the Beach area would save on major Residential property reconstruction; but it would not seriously reduce these inflationary Price rises, which are more affected by interruptions of Production.

Tornados have only about half the yearly impact to the American Economy, possibly far less. The reason lies in the limited area of Tornado effect. Tornados have only minimal effect upon Plant facilities, not possessing the capacity to lift heavy items. Plant operations are often back online within hours. Agricultural production remains relatively unaffected, except for the effects of Hail on Plant and Animal life, and the destruction of Agricultural equipment. Tornados rarely contain the Rainfall necessary to create Flood Conditions, in and of Itself. Lesser storms have even less impact. The losses from Tornados can be equated to the accelerated rate of Depreciation of Capital, including Residential property; and of course, the loss of Productive Labor assets. Tornados and Storms are a Human disaster, not an Economic disaster.

Floods are estimated to affect a possible Six percent of American territory every Year. Improper placement of Residential housing has vastly increased the Property loss of these Floods; the improper placement driven by Land values, increasing with Population density. Loss of residential housing, vehicle transport, and replacement of Road and Railway constitute the greatest losses of flooding; not forgetting the loss of Productive Labor assets. The Inflationary pricing comes basically from accelerated Capital depreciation, and delays of Transport schedules. The major difference, like Hurricanes, Floods take much longer to clean up after; significantly reducing Production levels during the Period of the Cleanup.

Drought stands as the last major natural disaster to affect the Economy. It has two real impact expressions on the Economy. The First is the loss of Agricultural Production. Much mention made of the Dust Bowl of the 1930s, where United States Agricultural Production dropped to less than half it's previous levels. Modern Agriculture has moved since that Period to the provision of Irrigation to arable land. The limit to Agricultural Economic planning remains a Time limitation: there must be a set level of Agricultural produce raised per year, else there will not be just huge Food prices increases; there will be moderate to advanced malnutrition. Irrigation of arable lands provide an increased minimum level of Agricultural production in the Short-run; but Water sources, River, Dam, and Underground basin, will be consumed under conditions of sustained Drought. The inflationary price of Irrigation is the Depreciation rate of this Agricultural equipment, plus the increasing Salinity of the arable land. All addition of neutralization elements to correct the Salinity are wholly inflationary.

There exists another potent force exhibiting itself under conditions of Agricultural production losses; this is the practice of Hoarding. Major shortages of Food supplies, both Human and Animal, can cause a real price increase of up to 1200%; before there is a drop in Consumer Demand because of inability to pay. Hoarding can halve the time required to reach malnutrition levels for some Consumers, by creating inflationary price levels up to 1200% in and of itself. More on Product Hoarding will come in a later Chapter; suffice it to say, Black Markets cause a worsening of Conditions of shortage.

The second impact of Drought comes in Water supply reductions. Population density produces every increasing demands for Water. Changing Weather patterns, due to Global Warming or to natural climatic cycles, alter the levels of Rainfall. Some Meteorologists suggest We are entering a Warming cycle, based on a periodic Planetary heating and cooling. Others claim it is Ozone-depletion Gases. The rationale does not matter; prediction does. Depth of Cool cycles in the Planet's history have generated a metamorphose of regions like the Sahara Desert into a resemblance of the American Great Plains. Historical Heat cycles have caused those same Great Plains to resemble the Sahara desert. Weather predictions state a real Heat cycle will not be evident for another Thousand Years, if it comes. Beginning changes could already be present; and the greatest initial evidence of those Changes would come as milder Winters and wetter Summers. Many are already citing the loss of Snowfall over the previous Thirty years. This shortage of Snowfall has deep Economic impact, as Water reservoirs generally receive almost Seventy percent of their Water from Snow.

The effect on Inflationary Market pricing is only beginning to be seen. Snowfall exhibits far greater retention capacity on Agricultural lands as Rainfall. Less than a quarter of every Inch of Rainfall is retained as moisture in the Soil; the rest fills Rivers and Streams as runoff. Almost one-half of an Inch of Snow will be absorbed, because of the slow rate of melt. Modern American Agricultural methods with heavy fertilizer and thick planting require at least forty absorbed Inches per year, else Farmers find some burn of Plant life. Irrigation can only replace around 12 Inches of absorbed moisture under current Irrigation methods per year. Irrigation cannot even replace this amount, unless Snow and Rain replace Water levels in the Basins. Reversion to planting and fertilization methods of pre-1940s would set a Production schedule for Agricultural Products creating some rate of malnutrition, because of Population density.

The inflationary price impact of such an alteration would consist of a tripling of Food prices, and Conversion to high-protein, Labor-intensive, high-yield human Foods. The Author speculates Rice Production could be introduced along the River valleys of America; and produce as much Rice; as this Country currently produces of Wheat. This would take Irrigation as well; but it would be soak Irrigation accomplished by half the current River flows. Planting such Foods as Potatoes, Radish, Soybeans, and Cucumbers on land currently planted to Corn and Milo;

could triple the effectiveness of current Irrigation methods, and produce over twice the Yield. The production of Chicken, Turkey, and Fish
stocks remains almost a third again as Food efficient; because larger
animals consume almost half of Feed in body maintenance, rather than
weight gain. Moderate Drought conditions over a sustained Period of
Ten or more years; would force these Food Production alterations.

The Price picture of Moderate Drought over sustained Period, can
really depress; it depresses even more, as certain indications show a
Thirty percent likelihood of such an Event within the next Fifty years.
Beef and Pork prices rise by Six Hundred Percent, while Production levels drop by Forty percent. Chicken, Turkey, and raised Fish will double
in Price, while Production will quadruple. The price of Wheat-flour
Bread will rise by 300%, while Production drops by Thirty percent.
Radish and Rice breads will make up for the Short-fall of Bread, though
at twice the Price of Wheat bread Today. The Consumption of Potatoes
and Radishes will make up half of the Individual Diet; Rice will produce
half of the Protein in the Diet. Potatoes, Radishes, and Cucumbers will
double in Price, as their Production triples. Fruit grown on Trees will
make up Ten percent of the Diet, as Irrigation of Trees is very efficient;
though the Price of this Fruit will double. Vine grown berries will rise
by 800% in Price, as Irrigation and water use of such Plants is very inef-
ficient. Ocean Fish will probably be the cheapest form of Protein,
though will rapidly rise, as Fish stocks deplete. The impact on both
Prices and Dietary habit will be very striking; Food diversity will shrink,
and remain shrunken with Water supply reduction.

The Picture for Extreme Drought belongs to a Draconian vision of
Hell. Many Sensationalist Authors, of which this Author is One, con-
sider the increase in Population density as nothing short of Suicide. A
halving of Rain and Snowfall for two consecutive years, would lead to
Water rationing beyond imagination. Water would be cut off at Public
Mains to any residential housing, Individuals would be allowed One
Gallon of Bottled Water per day, Public laundries and Showers would

use filtered recycled water, Portable toilets would sit on every residential street corner, and the Government would advocate the drinking of Beer as less wasteful than plain water. Twenty percent of current American production would cease, because it is profitable only using a water-wash process. American restaurants would charge you more a glass of water, than for a cup of Coffee, Coke, or Milk. Major Cities would spend Billions for reclamation plants, to reclaim Water from Dirty Water and Sewage. Game Wardens, Park Rangers, and Road maintenance personnel would be diverted to detection and arrest of Water thieves invading Public-owned reservoirs, lakes, rivers, and Ponds. Dehydration could easily claim 100,000 victims a Week.

Drought stands as the most viable threat to American society; it is far more likely than Nuclear War. An American Today stands a Eleven times greater chance of dying from Drought conditions, than any Terrorist attack. He stands at twice as much risk from Drought, as from a co-worker going Postal, and shooting him. Americans are in a Gamble to see what will kill them first; some undetected Pollution or Plague with delayed Period of physical expression, or death from Drought conditions. Neither is very likely to occur; Moderate Drought of sustained Period in not a question of if, only when. The lifestyle of All will change at this Point. One has only to study the lifestyles of Indian cities like Calcutta, Bombay, or New Delhi. Hundreds of Thousands, if not Millions, live in the Streets there; none have access to anything but potable water. Increasing Population density, along with Water shortage; brings a similar lifestyle to Millions of Americans, though they may retain their homes.

A final shortage of Resource We face is a shortage of Labor; though it is not that perceived by Business interests; who are only concerned by the availability of cheap labor, at the Wage levels they would desire to pay. Business interests continue to be the staunchest supporters of Immigration. The concern for an Economist comes with the decrease in the employees of Trades occupations. The percentage skilled Trade labor has been going down consistently for years, while the average age of Worker has been rising. Numbers of Doctors and Dentists increase far faster than do Carpenters and Plumbers. Construction companies find it impossible to hire competent help, or High School graduates interested in Apprenticeship. Business continually pushes the Romance of Trucking, to minimize personal Transport costs; by the creation of Owner-operator Truckers with one vehicle, who can be hired at marginal rates because of their need for Cargo. All other Trades suffer as a consequence.

The turn to high-tech weaponry in the Military, has lead to a vast reduction of trained personnel with Tradecraft MOS. The Military produced almost Forty percent of all trained Trades personnel some Thirty years ago, when Draftees made up over fifty percent of the Force. Trade-trained personnel are over-whelming retained by the Military Today, for full careers in the Service. This is because the Military provides better Pay, Housing, Medical, and Retirement packages for such Personnel, than does the Private Sector. They will not exit the Military, without considerable incentive.

Two-year Colleges (i.e. Community Colleges) attempt to make up for the trained Trade shortfall. The trouble comes in the fact trained Graduates make up less than half of the previous Military-trained personnel of long ago years, though the Population has increased dramatically. A minor insult must be inserted by the Author at this point; they seem to possess about a Twenty Percentile drop in I.Q. from the military-trained predecessors. This, at least, from hand-on experience at the minimum. They effectively require almost six times the supervision as military-trained, for a period of two years of Employment. A greater recruitment for these occupations contains little hope; they have neither the benefits or the Glamor of Software programing or Health service.

The upshot from the Inflationary price structure appears the payment of almost Sixty percent more Overtime in the Construction industry, than is economically viable. Remember Construction has traditionally always worked a Fifty-hour Week; a major incentive to trained Workers who relied on the increased Earnings. The Construction average Workweek, though, has increased to 54 hours during Ten months of the Year; and Workers are not laid off in the Winter Months, as it is too hard to recruit trained Labor after layoff. The introduction of the Community College graduates to this Workforce, has lowered Construction quality by an estimated Eleven percent. The aging of such trained Workers means Productivity levels have dropped in the Industry.

Other Tradecraft are suffering as well; the average Education level of retail store workers has been dropping for the last ten years. Bartenders, waitresses, domestic maids, and delivery personnel are dropping in Educational level; or consisting of Students managing a part-time job. All of these occupations have Wage levels determined to be below standard Economic model settings; none have viable Retirement or Medical benefits. The current Business trend to abandon the Workers without Medical coverage, retirement pension, or even Vacation time means there will be continued degradation of these occupations.

Chapter VI:
Economic Misallocation

◆

Government mal-regulation presents vast chance for distortion of the pricing mechanism. There is first and foremost the Traditional claim of the cause of Inflation; the printing of Currency instead of applying taxes to defray Government expenses. Rarely does this Practice occur because Political Leadership's ill will, most often due to simple Governing incompetence; where tax collection becomes failure, in terms of the Time element. An excellent example would be the post-WW I Weimar Republic of Germany. The Allies demanded Germany pay reparations for the War; these Reparations were demanded in raw materials and Product. Germany's domestic economy was struggling to re-establish it's viability, and return to Production levels of pre-War. This generated huge inflationary pressure in the Resource Recovery market. German business passed along these higher prices to their Customers, and the inflationary price spiral began. It was produced by the huge resource draft syphoned out of the German Economy.

The German Government itself had to purchase in the inflationary market, competing for necessities against private Consumers. The German Tax system, though, was geared to tax collections gathered after Monthly accounting had been completed. The Weimar Government immediately to lose sufficiency of tax receipts to meet Government expenditures; starting initially at about Five percent per Month. The Political leadership found it impossible to raise tax percentages in the German Parliament; after the huge tax burden of the War years, revolutionary sentiment and unrest continuing at high levels. They started to print Currency to meet their commitments. This only fed the Inflation; before the end of the hyper-inflation, levels of Inflation reached over Two Million percent a Month. It became so bad; Business would only produce heavy-ticket items, if Customers would agree to pay the prevailing Price of the Product some Thirty days after delivery; Businesses needing to purchase replacement resources and materials before payment.

Any degree of Inflation which operates at a faster rate than the Tax Collection system; will incite this facility of Governmental stupidity. All it takes is Tax receipts degrading by inflationary prices, before those receipts can reach the Government Treasury. Governments have no other option, but to print Money. The only other preventive consists of such onerous Tax increases, Consumer demand in the Market is sharply reduced. This effort is wasted, if Consumers become used to the Inflationary spiral; they simply estimate they will make sufficient revenue in the following Month, to pay for this Month's tax. The only curative once hyper-inflation has started; consists of trading in another Currency which is stable, the United States Dollar exercising this constraint on hyper-inflation on many occasions. Tax agencies simply demanding tax payment in the foreign Currency, and Government paying for it's necessities in it's own Currency; until the Government in question can buy back enough of it's own Currency, to make it stable again.

Governmental printing of Money is far from the only source of Inflation generated by Government action. One of the great understandable instances is the impact of Tariffs. Normal Economic model priced Products and raw materials prevented from normal pricing purchase, by taxes placed upon these Goods. Government often placed on such Goods, to protect developing native industries from established foreign industries. This can be sound, if there is major debt-structure differentials between the developing native industry, and the established foreign industry. The native industry could not Price compete, because of the added cost of the debt-financing. Developing industries cannot endure Price wars with lower-production cost established foreign Competitors. Such Tariffs seem economically sound; they are not!

Tariffs disturb the normal price structuring of all Products associated with the tariff Product; Component parts, raw materials, Competing products, and Complimentary products all have prices shifted off normal level pricing. Component parts and raw materials find themselves with higher Prices, because of an enhanced demand on them through protected Product production. Competing goods find a lessened Consumer demand; causing less Profitability, if not lower prices. Complimentary Goods find a higher demand and higher prices; but an over-capitalization than called for, because of over-share profitability.

The proper Economic way to subsidize native industry remains the practice of Tax eliminations for the industry, until a certain level of yearly sales is reached. Both Tariffs and Tax eliminations retain the potential for Government mal-regulation. Newly developing industries hardly have the funds for political lobbying; they almost never able to influence Governments to provide protection, in terms of Tariffs or tax elimination. Tariffs and tax eliminations always going to Those who can afford Political lobbying, established industries remain the only recipients of Tariff benefits and tax eliminations. This inflates the price structure, with over-capitalization of the industry, subsidiary raises in price by others to pay for their heightened taxes, over-draft of resources price increases, and price rises associated only with a Government-sanctioned monopoly position in the Market through lowered costs of production. Any potential Economic gains to a Nation by such economic measures, are always destroyed by Political corruption.

Tax Credits stand as the greatest impact Political corruption to affect the pricing structure. Only established industries can reach the Government, through political lobbying and campaign contributions. Tax credits for Investment by Business is One major distortion of the price structure. Tax Credits work only for established industries as a viable option; translated, if One can make huge profits, the Business can keep his investors satisfied and get a huge decrease in his tax rate by investing in more high-profit ventures. Small Business is quick to swallow the concept of Tax Credits, because the Business can deduct their recapitalization schedule from their taxes. They believe they are making a huge windfall gain. Nothing could be further from the Truth.

Tax Credits drain support for an economically effective tax alternative, which is a graduated Corporate Income Tax rate. Such a graduated rate of tax would tax the more heavily capitalized Businesses are a higher rate than lesser businesses. All organizations would still be able to deduct their costs of Production, Distribution, and Sales. The difference would be impacting the tax on Businesses with ability to pay. Small Businesses could pay one-quarter of what is currently paid, while large Conglomerates would pay triple the actual tax rate now paid. An alternative method of understanding of this Issue can come with the statement, Microsoft and GM both invest more Capital per year, than 800 American averaged-size businesses of total-value capitalization; all without spending a cent on taxes. A correct tax rate on Corporations in this Country could replace the revenues of 160,000 averaged-sized businesses now paying the tax. This Work, though, is a piece on Inflation, not a tirade to change the Tax Code; therefore, it must be said the excessive taxation of small business in this Country cause an overall inflationary price rise in the Market. Large Corporations over-capitalize as much as Forty percent, inciting a further overall inflationary price Three percent above normal; to maintain normal profitability.

Government regulatory practice can also incite much inflationary price structuring. Government safety regulations introduced since 1965 increased the overall cost to Business of almost Twenty percent of Operating Cost. This has brought an estimated inflationary price structuring of Nine percent overall in the Market. The cost of enforcing the safety regulations now exceed Two Billion dollars per year. The awards of Civil suits against Industry prior to 1965 cost less than Two Billion, even when adjusted for Inflation. Awards for Civil Suits against Industry for Industrial accidents exceed the Awards largesse prior to 1965, even when adjusted for Inflation. Reductions in Industrial accident rates, equated in lost Labor hours; do not even equal the increases in Awards, let alone the Two Billion dollars for the various programs. All Economists, as least all the Author talked with, concur that only fear of Damage Awards propel Industry to improve it's safety equipment; the spottiness of OSSHEA enforcement and impediment of regulations to required Production quotas, make Government regulation unacceptably marginal.

An adequate replacement could be Federal legislation specifying all Damage awards be limited to multiples of a Worker's income–not to exceed Fifty–plus all medical needs. This legislation would have to insist all industrial accidents have to be settled by Court action; at no cost to the Worker, Court-appointed Counsel for the Worker paid along with all Court costs by the Employer, and the Employer would be burdened with proof that the Accident was not his fault. The Legislation would allow deduction of all costs for the Employer. The Legislation would also call for a fine of a Worker of up to Six months wage or salary, if the Claim was found to be completely spurious. The Legislation would entail all Counsel could represent the Case only for specified Salary set by the Judge, and paid by the Employer. The Legislation should also state that the Award could be appealed to a Superior Court of Appeal; but the Award had to be paid in the interim, or within Twenty working days of the Court.

The current trend in Congress runs to forbidding Civil Action on the part of Injured against Businesses. Seating Republicans find potential benefit in altering the basic nature of American jurisprudence; mainly because of the extreme sums granted to their Campaigns from Soft Money. Most Commentators will not go so far as to call Soft Money, Bakash Bribery; yet it is what it is. Almost Forty years of it's intensive use has caused a vast skew to the Pricing mechanism; this Author believes it causes over a 23% inflationary price increase of overall pricing. It is assured legislation against the Individual's right to Sue will lead to further vast dislocations to the pricing system.

Specific Agency legislation or regulatory action also produces profound inflationary impact. Federal action by Congress allowed States to set their own Speed Limits. This and following State action lead directly to a 24% increase in the consumption of Fuel. It further reduced the schedule of recapitalization of Transport trucks by almost Two years. The number of Truck Accident deaths increased by about 14%. The increased milage has led to assumed exhaustion in Truckers to increased by 41%. The lowered freight rates in Truck Transport led to a Four percent reduction of Train system Cargo. These lowered rates have also put an additional 300,000 Truckers on the Road, with an average of 1.7 years less experience. Motor and Brake wear comes at almost four times the rate as under the 55 mile an hour Speed Limit. The Congestion of Road systems have increased almost Six percent from the increased traffic, as figured by more driver miles per year. The impact on the pricing system from the higher Speed Limits are hard to detail; it is estimated Fuel costs have increased by $.07 a gallon from the unnecessary increased usage per Transport mile. Road maintenance costs increased by an estimated Twelve percent. Truck maintenance costs have increased an assumed $1240 per vehicle, over the life expectancy of the Vehicle; life expectancy of Trucks reduced by Two years, or a price tag of $12,000 per vehicle. The transfer of freight from Trains to Trucks is estimated to cost about $3.7 Billion a year increase to the Total Transport cost of the Nation per year. The savings to

Individual Businesses from the lower freight rates is estimated not to exceed $300 Million a year.

The Federal Aviation Agency (FAA) refuses to limit airport access to Business, because of pressure of Congress. The FAA does this even though the risk of Air Accident has increased by a factor of 370%, and ground Accident has increased by 830%. Congress pressures the FAA because Airlines and Air Transport provides over $100 Million of Soft Money per year to Congressional Candidates. The risk of Accident should not enter this Discussion, through having little impact on the pricing system. The increased Traffic does have a real impact on the price system; through the fact the Traffic is economically unviable.

Passengers are led to risk their lives by flying, because of Advertising inducement of flying being faster than other mode of Transport. Train transportation maintains it's lead as the most comfortable form of Transport for Passengers. The properly Capitalized Train system of the 1940s and 1950s could deposit a Passenger at his destination in 160 percent of the Time, which Airlines do Today. The saving in Transport Cost per Passenger, even with Recapitalization of the Train system, would be about $.17 per mile. The saving in terms of transferring Airfreight to Trains would be about $.037 per mile. The savings in transferring Truck freight to Trains would be even greater, some $.061 per mile-ton. Half the Runway maintenance costs of Airports could be saved, if Air traffic was reduced by Thirty percent.

Governmental refusal to establish a Civil Service Quartermaster Corps, opting for nationally awarded long-term Contracts; cost the Federal Agencies almost Thirty percent above Market cost in purchasing. Mandated Military contracts for other than weapon systems cost the Military an estimated Two percent of their Budget per year. This long-term contracting increases the inflationary pricing of the Market by almost One percent, due to the largesse of Federal purchasing, and increased Taxes raised to pay the excesses of long-term contracting. The total refusal of Washington bureaucrats to devolve Authority to

Regional leadership; costs an inflationary price increase of almost Three percent. This comes from delays in Decision-making, insistence on Uniform payments throughout the Country, and interference regulation.

The size of the Federal Civil Service, plus the Military, projects a Scenario where the Federal Government, itself, through it's skewed operation; cause an estimated inflationary price increase of Four percent overall, not counting Military War Production. State Government operations can be expected to provide an equivalent inflationary increase per year. The Corruption of State and Local Contract awards add Two percent more Inflation. Soft Money, in and of itself, undoubtedly causes a One percent rise in the Inflation rate; due to the amount of funds spend on advertising and Mail, for no economic reason. The loss of productive labor resources in economically inappropriate programs provide another percent of inflationary pricing.

Chapter VII:
Product Hoarding

◆

This Concept seems simple, but economically provides for huge skewing of Price schedules. Sophisticated forms of Product hoarding develop what is known as the Black Market. Everyone has heard of Black Markets, almost no one can define the term. A simplified logical explanation of Black Markets will be given; all are based on product scarcity. This scarcity can be actual or relative; based upon the real production levels of products. Scarcity must be defined in economic terms: Scarcity simply being the inability of Productive capacity to replace consumed product inside the time frame desired by Consumers. Scarcity can be absolute, in that Productive capacity cannot produce sufficient product; Scarcity is relative if Productive capacity is sufficient, but the distribution of product has been slowed or interrupted. Either will induce some segment of Consumers to pay more for Product; and induce Suppliers to provide Product at the higher prices.

The time frame holds the critical importance in the development of Product hoarding of all types. Simple threat of Productive or Distributive disruption leads Consumers to stock up on specific products; thinking to head off possible personal shortages of said products. This personal stockpiling can introduce inflationary pricing, even where there is sufficient supply. The increased short-run Consumer demand generally incites an inflationary price increase from 10-400%; no actual shortage need exist. The condition may continue for sustained periods of time without shortage, as the higher pricing and threat of shortage signals further Consumers to stockpile Product. Periods of up to Two years have been witnessed, where there was no actual shortage; the greatest example probably being Car and Truck tires during the Second World War, where productive capacity was sufficient by 1943 for both domestic and War production, but where the Black Market continued to sell 40% of all tires until 1946. The image of time frame governs both Consumer and Supplier.

Consumers remain relatively undifferentiated in a Black Market, the great difference among them being the urgency of their need. The Suppliers in a Black Market, though, must exhibit very specialized function characteristics. Suppliers must have enhanced access to Black Market products, determined by position. They must possess contacts within the Production process for continual operation; or contacts within the Distribution network for temporary operation. What type of position held controls the ability to regulate the pricing structure. Military Company Sargents in Vietnam were able to charge almost full Stateside price for Beer to the troops, though the Beer was supposed to be free to the troops. They did this for years, setting their own price for the Beer; because they had absolute charge of Company supply. Black Marketeers in Warsaw or Moscow cannot set prices, because they cannot limit competitors; all must relay on Mules to purchase in the Western countries, and transport to the Black Market.

The Military Company Sargents of the Vietnam era could maintain the Black Market, though there was no actual shortage. Black Marketeers of Eastern Europe remain an impactive element in Eastern European economies, because of inability of domestic economies to produce quantity and quality of Product equal with Western European economies. The Vietnam Black Market of the War years was a relative scarcity maintained by the ability to control supply. The Black Market of Eastern Europe is an absolute, or actual, scarcity maintained by inadequacy of Productive capacity. The functioning of relative and absolute scarcity Black Markets vary in several important aspects: Relative scarcity Black Markets can only be sustained by positional interruption of the time frame of distribution; absolute scarcity Black Markets entails some segment of the population will not be supplied with Product, suffering duress. Absolute scarcity Black Markets always insist on some level of Violence, to provide for protection of Product from theft. The most violent absolute scarcity Black Market in History is that of illegal drugs; a forum where over half of the Suppliers are traditionally killed by Consumers or fellow Competitors.

Relative scarcity Black Markets generally never incur inflationary pricing over 400%; and often introduced for low sustained profits to the Black Market operators. A prime example of sustained Black Markets are Utilities and Cable companies in the United States. They maintain permanent inflationary prices due to their monopoly position in an area. They charge over normal costs and profits, but under incentive levels which would result in competitive systems. This averages approximately Nine percent for Utilities, and about 17% for Cable companies. Telephone companies face stiff competition since Government-mandated breakup. They return to relative scarcity Black Market pricing by inconsistency of product pricing; with switching their Customer base to higher pricing schedules without notice of change to the Consumer. The major criteria for such relative scarcity Black Markets relies on Public lack of knowledge of mode of operation.

The insidiousness of such relative scarcity Black Markets lies in the continual drain of the Consumer dollar through the inflationary pricing. Utilities, Telephone, and Cable TV companies combine to overcharge their Customers on average between $30-7000 per month, based on Customer consumption patterns. Consumption patterns are fairly predictable in income levels of American society. Inflationary pricing of these relative scarcity Black Markets are set to charge the average

Customer some Two to Three percent of his gross income per year. This is not normal Profit and Cost charging; it is in excess of that average Six percent of normal income. A rough estimate by the Author would suggest such overcharging costs the average Customer some Four percent of their actual Income tax payments. Another view of the practice would say these Companies make approximately $230 per employee over and above normal costs and wages, solely due to relative scarcity Black Market pricing for provided Goods.

The impact on the overall pricing structure cannot be easily determined; yet it must exceed Three percent of the total Wholesale cost of all products on the Market. Current trends in Production products drift towards energy-intensive products; insisting the overall impact from these relative scarcity Black Markets will continue to grow. Replacement of human labor with machinery brings added cost from these Black Markets. Consumer products also use increasing energy in operation; increasing the inflationary profits of these Companies. The privatization of Utilities has only increased this Black Market profiteering.

The effect of these Black Market relative scarcity operators does not stop here, when considering inflationary pricing. The high Profits expressed by these Companies skew the total Price structure, through inciting other businesses to match their Profits; to forestall raids on their investment Capital (i.e. Stock value loss). Workers in these relative scarcity Black Markets perceive the high Profit ratios, and demand wage increases and benefits packages in excess of usual labor rates. Black Market operators bow to these demands, to keep Profits flowing without interruptions. Fellow workers in other industries witness these increased benefits, and insist on the same for themselves. Industries which can provide this labor packaging, does so; in the interest on smooth labor relations. This leads to a two-tier labor stratum, split between high-tech industries which can pass on labor costs to final product pricing, and the rest of the economy industries which cannot.

The above would not have been mentioned, except for it's effect on the pricing structure. High-tech industry labor has greater viability in the Pricing structure, than does their counterparts in the rest of the economy. They are almost always joined by Government Civil Service employees. This actually means a drop in purchasing power for the rest of the labor force, with a consequent drop in Consumer Demand. The resultant reports as lessened impact on the Price structure, than the inflationary pricing would inflict. This is because the rest of labor force has to endure the majority of the inflationary pricing. The reportage of inflationary pricing does not reflect the lower Standard of Living, for the majority of the labor force. Workers in the rest of the labor force actually suffers a loss of wage. Their employer businesses also raise their pricing, so these Workers lose almost twice the pay increase of high-tech industries' Workers in less buying power. Drops in the Standard of Living equate to about 80% of the wage increase to high-tier Workers minus the wage increases to the rest of the Economy, on a per-employee basis.

Here resides the most serious affect of all Black Markets: Consumer Demand drops because of the inflationary pricing, while the huge profits of the Suppliers are not translated into Consumer Demand. Such profits are used to engage in further criminal activity, to support Vice, or as investment capital in further legitimate industry. Productive industry suffers from lowered production, normal Wage increases are eaten up by inflationary pricing, and Vice disorders the normal functioning of society. The Tax base is eroded overall, while the demand for welfare services increase dramatically. The return to normal production schedules comes only with long-term price increases; due to increased Capitalization costs, higher demanded Wages, and resistence of business to return to normal pricing.

The existence of absolute, or actual, scarcity Black Markets are much worse in effect on the price structure. A significant segment of Consumers have been deprived of the necessities of their own productivity, so there is

actual loss in their production. The Goods and Services provided by
this segment of the Consuming labor force has been disturbed, with
loss of Wages and Profits. The lessened productivity causes an increase
in pricing for these Goods and Services. Return to full production for
these laborers may be impossible or long-term, so the inflated price
structure may have a residual permanence. The increased pricing never
reflects a profitability in such Production, so there is minimal funding
for recapitalization. Full production will often be delayed for a
Generation, awaiting a new supply of Labor. This can cause inflationary
pricing to become permanent.

The Industries whose products made up the Black Market equally
suffer. Black Markets never return the higher Profits to the Industry, so
recapitalization to meet Demand is always delayed. Such industries
often suffer from reduced Profit per product ratios, during operation
of Black Markets. This comes from increased operational costs associated with the dislocation. They are faced with increased resource costs
due to Black Market induced pricing, lowered employee capacity, and
decayed recapitalization schedules from higher maintenance and
equipment costs. A major factor of loss will always be theft of product;
where employees make unauthorized sales to Black Marketeers without payment, as supplement to their own income. Disintegration of
the production process through inability to maintain overhead costs
will often occasion. Return to Full Production means employment of
massive security measures at inflationary employment costs. These
security services destroy normal Profits, and disrupt recapitalization
schedules. Most such Industries find Production Costs to increase by a
factor of Thirty percent or more.

The greatest impact to the Price structure comes from the overall
Economy. Black Market inflationary pricing leads business throughout
the affected Economy, to double or triple their Profit ratios to meet
current operating expenses. The final elimination of the Black Market
will return distribution to normal; but does not automatically pressure

normal businesses. Businessmen will not volunteer Profit diminishments, except through the introduction of competition. Existent Competition are operating on the same price scheduling levels, and are equally opposed to Profits diminishments. Reservoir Funds have been drained by the precedent Black Market inflationary pricing, and new competition seems unlikely. Normal business begins to engage in relative scarcity Black Market pricing.

The engagement in relative scarcity Black Market pricing by normal business, if not forestalled by Government intervention, will continue for a minimum period which reestablishes the financial reserves of the normal business leadership, plus introduction of effective price competition. This can become an incredibly long period duration, when considering heavy capitalization industries. Tire companies in the United States sought to maintain higher than normal prices for tires, after World War II. They had been producing under stringent production price controls and Government contracts during the War. Black Market prices for tires reached 600% of the price they were allowed to charge by 1944.

The Tire companies attempted to maintain a third of that price after they were freed from Government controls. The heavy Capitalization of tire production precluded easy entrance in the Market for Competitors. Competition arrived from Overseas source only in the late 1960s; these Competitors also desirous of the high prices on American sale of tires. Most Economists would agree normal pricing off of production costs did not start until after the Oil Embargo of 1973, though the inflationary pricing share had been dropping slowly since the end of the Korean War in 1953.

Leaving the effects of Black Markets on inflationary pricing, Author and Reader can now define a more coherent structure of Product Hoarding. The practice always occurs when Consumers develop expectation production or distribution of some product, or series of products, will not fulfill future needs; this perception may be actual, imaginary, or elicited by positional corruption. The Product Hoarding worsens the situation, and can actually create a shortage when one was not previously present. A Black Market development is dependent on two conditions; first, an actual shortage must be present–whether actual or elicited, and secondly, the product or products must be of such desirability multiple factor pricing can be demanded. Black Market pricing always drains the financial reserves of the Consuming market, and leads to failures of recapitalization for the Producers of the Goods.

Relative scarcity Black Market pricing possess much resistence to elimination; a current example lies with Microsoft, whose inflationary pricing has withstood proposed action by the Justice Department. Utilities and Oil Companies continually cite increasing costs of production to cancel anger at scarcity inflationary pricing. Automobile companies have developed Consumer Finance structures to deflect criticism of inflationary pricing. The Author uses a short rule to determine use of relative scarcity inflationary pricing: Check the Corporate Executive benefits program; the cost of Corporate management will invariably be increasing faster (at a higher percentage) than any other cost of the Corporate production. It is indicative of relative scarcity inflationary pricing, if Management cost exceeds Eight percent of the total Operating Costs of a Corporation or Business. Management costs of Computer Tech industries are running at approximately 23% of Operating Costs; Oil Company Management costs are currently running at approximately 17% of Operating Costs; and Utility Management costs are running at approximately 14% of all Operating Costs.

Contrary to the expectations of Stockholders in such Companies, there is little of this inflationary pricing which devolves on themselves. Corporate Executive Salary and Incentive programs eat up almost all inflationary pricing. Stockholders at most save the cost of Management, through the use of inflationary pricing. Study of Corporate salaries and incentive programs find a magnitude of a minimum of 95% of inflationary pricing, and a maximum of 120% of the inflationary pricing values. Stockholder dividends are estimated only after inflationary pricing profits have been distributed amongst Corporate management.

The cost of relative scarcity Black Market pricing in this Country, from 1983 to the Present, can be roughly estimated around Eleven percent of the total cost of purchases in the Industries using inflationary pricing. The cost to the total Market can be estimated to be almost Three percent of the total cost of Products purchased. Almost all of this amount has been distributed between 38,000 members of the Corporate structure in the United States. Many have wondered at the quick Fortunes gained in the last Boom, though these gains have been coming to Corporate management since Congress mandated IRS accounting changes to accommodate Corporations in 1983. Explanation remains easy, though numeral proof is hard to collect.

This Work, though, remains a study of Inflation. It is sufficient to state without exact Model proof, relative scarcity Black Market inflationary pricing accounts for Eighty percent of the inflationary pressure existent in the American economy. All prices have raised an inflationary two percent per year simply to purchase these Black Market provided products. Adjusted Wage levels of Labor cannot be determined without extensive modeling, yet this Author believes there has been a 14% drop in real Wages because of inflationary pricing since 1983. Stockholders have been boxed into a set return on their investment, averaging Eleven percent since 1983 if Production was actually showing a profit of 22%; while their purchases have gone up at the same rate as all Consumers in the Market. The previous statement leads into a discussion advanced by the next Chapter; discussion of where almost half of the above inflationary pressure comes from.

Chapter VIII: Profits Hoarding

———————— ◆ ————————

Profits Hoarding consists of the simple practice long understood; Companies and Industries use their monopoly position to enjoy higher Profit ratios by gouging the Consumers of their products. The economic formulation for the practice contains more complexity, because it must show the effect of the activity on the rest of the Economy. A simple economic explanation would say Profits Hoarding causes other Companies and Industries to be under-capitalized through loss of Consumer share of the Market, determined by Dollar share of Consumer income. Like any simple reply given to convoluted issues, It confuses more than it illuminates. The purpose of this Chapter attempts edification of the Issue; possibly an unfortunate expectation of the Author.

Start must be made at the level of Corporate structure; an understanding of which is necessary for further discussion. Modern Corporations adopted a wide variety of Accounting procedures and techniques, accepted by the IRS after 1983. The first effect of the IRS acceptance was the ability to discharge two-thirds of their apparent yearly tax without payment. They were basically allowed to register use of their own operating funds as a Cost; simpler put, Corporations claimed use of their own funds was a Cost to themselves, and the IRS allowed such use as a genuine operating expense. Corporations could deduct their operating costs, but also their funds used to pay those operating costs, doubling functionally the deduction of their operating costs plus lost interest on the funds used. The rationale used for such deductions from the tax base was it was have cost them a like amount, if they had borrowed the funds from an outside source. The IRS was muscled by Congress to do this; Congress well-oiled by political contributions from Corporate America.

Corporate America altered to provide realism to the fiction. Almost half of Corporate America had already switched to Sector accounting by 1983, the rest rapidly followed. Sector accounting is the simple practice of decreeing separate departments, or separate Plants owned by the Corporation; are semi-autonomous Units. These Units must carry their own Operating Budget, possess their own amortization and recapitalization schedules, and maintain their own profitability. The Parent Corporation assumes the role of banker to the various Sectors; holding mythical mortgages, appointing Sector management, and setting Growth and recapitalization schedules. Each Sector is expected to pay for all it's expenses, pay for all Wages and salaries of the Sector, and meet the production, recapitalization, Growth, and Sales schedules set by the Parent Corporation. Each Sector (sells) it's product to other Sectors of the Parent Corporation, or to the Public.

Each Sector is expected to maintain approximately Twelve percent profitability; but never records such profit for tax purposes. This amount is used to fund recapitalization, Growth, or Mortgage repayments to the Parent Corporation. There has already been a maintenance of a 12% profit at Sector level; but neither Sector or Parent Corporation yet records a Profit. The Parent Corporation insists returns from each Sector is simply repayment for extension of Credit to the Sector, claiming Profits only if these repayment schedules have been exceeded; a practice carefully regulated by creation of new Sectors, or Sector expansion through extension of further Credit to Sectors. Corporate

reportage of Profits means those Profits plus the profits of the various
Sectors; a claim of 10% profitability on total Volume means a real Profit
of 22%. A Corporate reported loss invariably means a Profit ratio of
something more than 12%, but less than Corporate management
desire; stock dividends will not be paid.

Corporate financial viability is never in question, because of the
profitability of the various Sectors. Unprofitable Sectors are closed or
sold. Corporate management salaries and benefits continue to rise, and
Workers are laid off by claimed unprofitability, while Corporations
claim losses to the IRS; because of the fiction of mortgage extension to
the Sectors. Worker, Stockholder, and IRS remain unpaid. Price and
Growth schedules remain unaffected by the reported losses. Corporate
management fearing only replacement through Stockholder anger,
because of loss of dividends. Corporate Executive Stock Option incentives have even been known to increase in the face of reported
Corporate losses.

Stock Option incentives remain the means for Corporate management to profit from productivity; how it is done will shock even the
Stockholders who allow them. Stockholder dividends are carefully
boxed; never allowed to increase dramatically through upward revi-
sion of Growth schedules, and paid only off Profits reported by the
Parent Corporation. Stock option largesse resides on the exact expansion of the Corporate capital. Corporate Executive salaries are set for
the specific purpose of borrowing sufficient Credit to exercise those
Stock Options. The acquired Stock is immediately sold on the open
market, and re-invested to avoid tax. The Credit is paid off, and the
Executive has the added wealth. This is the foundation for the great
interest of Corporate management in maintaining Corporate Stock
prices. Normal Corporate Stockholders never benefit from Capital
growth; they simply get their dividends, if Corporate management
feels Profits were high enough to pay dividends. The only assurance of
stock dividend payment lies in the desire of Corporate management

to maintain high Stock prices to sell their acquired stock from Stock options.

Many may doubt the above analysis; the Author has often been accused of a skewed view of modern Corporate practice. The Author would refer the typical Stockholder to the largesse of percentage return, as compared to the largesse of Corporate growth for the proposed Stock. Your return is unlikely to increase at any time, while Corporate growth rates are at about three times your aggregate Stock dividends. Ownership is being transferred elsewhere, and expanding. Personal stock holdings face loss of operative control, and lessened share in the profitability of the Corporation. Stock Options of Management approach Three percent of total issued Stock of Corporations in many industries per year. Twenty years of operation will cut your voting power in half, and your profitability will not reflect the growth of the Corporation.

The above has little to do with Profit Hoarding per se; it is a simple mandate of information to grasp the operation of the greater problem, which is affectation of Prices in the greater Market. Profit Hoarding arrives in the economic situation by way of the claims of extension of Costs. Sector pricing uses the (mortgage) payments to the Parent companies as a Cost of operation; at amounts rising to one-third of the Price of products. It also insists on a Twelve percent profit on all Operating Costs, including the payments to the Parent Company. The mortgage payments to the Parent Company are a fiction; in reality, a profit on Production. This profit on Production is not Profit Hoarding; but the reserved 12% profit on the payments are most distinctly Profit Hoarding. The Parent Company maintains these payments are not profits of Production; but simply a return of extended Capital plus interest. The interest returned stands as the only Profit which the Parent Company records for tax purposes. The actual fact remains the entire payment is Profits on Production.

The question must be asked at this point: What is the exact level of Profit Hoarding? Normal Profits must be considered as the percentage of Operating Costs at the Sector level, including the recapitalization schedule; but not including the payments made to the Parent Company. Profits Hoarding consists of the entirety of payments made to the Parent Company; plus Twelve percent of those payments, charged by the Sector as profit on Operating Costs. Sector Accounting allows Corporations to claim a double use of Capital; while in fact, there has only been the singular use of capitalizing Production. This claim of double use allows Corporations to claim a double profit, though often not a exact doubling. Tax evasion is only a minor element in the economic equation; the practice has a heavy economic impact.

There remains the Corporate ability to heavily increase their Capital aggregation function; providing for Growth rates sometimes Five times greater, than achievable through Normal Profits operation. Almost all business would think to engage in such practice, except the practice has limitations. There must be limitation to Competition in the Industry involved, before such profits can be extracted. There remains only one effective limitation to competition, the production of heavily-capitalized production of high technology products. Two-thirds of the Economy cannot achieve the limitation necessary to generate the necessary Profit levels. The economic effect is that High-tech, heavily-capitalized Companies can achieve much higher Growth rates than the rest of the Economy. The major failure of the NASDEQ companies was attempts to use such Sector Accounting with inflated extraction of Profits, while the Capitalization levels were insufficient to limit entrance into competition.

A much heavier impact of Profits Hoarding using Sector Accounting with inflated extraction of Profits comes from movement of Product through the Production process itself. Products have to travel through various Sectors to reach Consumer purchase. Raw materials have to be purchased by the Purchasing Sector, they have to be transported to Production site by the Transportation Sector, the Production Sector may finish the Product or only produce parts, where the parts have to be transported to the Assembly Sector by the Transportation Sector, the Assembly Sector finishes the Product, which has to be transported to the Retail Sector by the Transportation Sector, where the Retail Sector sells to the Consumer with possible use of the Consumer Credit Sector. Each Sector insists on a 12% profit on operating costs which includes (mortgage) payments to the Parent Company. These payments to the Parent Company plus 12% of these payments considered as profits on operating costs by Sectors, were considered to be inflationary profits, or Profits Hoarding. Extended transmission through the Production process can mean that final price to the Consumer, means half or over of the price is Profits Hoarding. This devolves into a statement that the Consumer pays twice the Price for the Product, as he would under Normal Profits Production.

Production from the One-Third of the Economy engaged in Sector Accounting with inflated extraction of Profits, make up only about one-third of the Production purchased by the Consumer; but approximately eighty-five percent of the big-ticket items. A rough estimate would suggest that Consumers expend half their income on items produced by these industries. This suggests somewhere between Fifteen to Twenty-five percent of the Average Consumer income goes to provide the funding for this Profit Hoarding. An alternate view would say Consumers lose up to a quarter of their pay, or an amount greater than any actually pay for Income Tax. The final bill for Profits Hoarding is staggering!

The reflection on the Price structure, though, is not near as clear. There is clearly great inflationary pricing involved, up to a twenty per-cent rise in overall prices. There are intense deflationary effects on Prices as well. A Conservative estimate would place a Ten percent decrease in Production levels on the current level of Profits Hoarding. This must equate as around a 12 to 15% reduction on resource prices, as could be expected under Normal Profits Production schedules. This translates as a Two percent reduction of expected overall Prices.

Investments make up about twenty percent of the income of American Households. Profits Hoarding could be expected to have doubled this percentage, through guarantee of dividend payments and interest returns. Consumer debt, on the other hand, can be expected to have raised by one-third in magnitude, due to Profits Hoarding. Certainty cannot be found in effective evaluations, but it can be expected Consumers pay Fifteen percent more for all products, over purchase of like products produced by Normal Profits Production.

The effect on the Inflationary rate on the Economy contains another story. Profits Hoarding initially reduces inflationary pressure on the Resource Market; so there are immediate gains in deflationary pressure from Profits Hoarding. This, though, remains a short-run effect. Over half of the inflationary pressure felt in the Pricing structure comes from the Resource Market; Prices in this Market determined by shrinking levels of materials, and increasing costs of extraction. Initial use of Profits Hoarding reduces Resource use, therefore slows Price increases.

The insistence on Sector profitability on each level of the Production process has a counter-veiling adverse factor. Minor increase in the Resource Market resound as escalating price, at each level of insisted profitability. This means that the Resource price increase is activated at each level where profitability is estimated; a one percent Price increase in the Resource Market will mean a Five percent increase in resource cost, if profitability is incurred in five Sectors. Once the initial deflation-ary pressure of Resource-use reduction is run through; there will be a magnification effect on Resource price increases, due to Sector Accounting. The practice of Profits Hoarding, thereby, applies it's own inflationary pressure in the long-run.

The Economist must stay concerned with both the short-run, and the long-run; when considering Economic issues. Economic Production for the Industries capable of Profits Hoarding have been engaged in the prac-tice since the mid-Eighties. The deflationary pressures associated with Profits Hoarding may be assumed to have dissipated in the intervening interval. Production levels have been increasing dramatically in the last decade. One can assume Sector Accounting with extraction of inflationary profits exhibit full inflationary pressure. There is currently much evidence of Resource-pushed inflationary price increases, worsened by Profits Hoarding.

Every Economist must be concerned with Production levels, even those investigating Inflation. Production ability is not a consideration, what with the over-capitalization coming from Profits Hoarding. Corporations have maintained intense Investment schedules using Profits Hoarding; to avoid Government taxation of Profits, and to provide a method of financial transference to Corporate management through Stock Options. It is clear there exists under-utilization of current productive capacity, due to excessive conflicting competition at the Present. Production has become a function of Marketing, not of Capital accumulation.

Marketing faces much difficulty in the current Economic environment. Consumer debt stands higher than it has ever been, even when adjusted by increases in income levels. Tax relief, though attempted by the current administration, seems impossible without deficit spending by Government. Discretionary Consumer income will not increase markedly from this venue. Wage increases, even for productivity, seem destined to fall victim to energy price increases. Extension of further Consumer Credit, especially with heavy Government deficit spending, carries high risk of massive Inflation. The economic situation is complicated by the fact the Age-quotient of durable and semi-durable products owned by Consumers is as low as the mid-1960s, and possibly as low as the late 1940s. This allows Consumers to delay purchases for a 3-6 year period, under financial constraint. There remains no un-exploited Consumption Market, either here or Overseas.

Sector Accounting with extraction of inflated Profits makes soft Consumer Demand much worse. Resource generated inflation becomes magnified under Series level profitability accounting, as mentioned earlier. Consumer debt levels are also magnified by factor levels. Certain mandatory purchase levels present are heavily affected by Profits Hoarding; the most notable being Fuel, Housing, Transportation, Communication, Electricity, and Food. Agriculture is not viable for Profits Hoarding, but all of it's component operating costs come directly from Profits Hoarding industries. This matrix means under adverse economic conditions, Profits Hoarding Companies and industries absorb almost all Consumer discretionary buying power. Discretionary purchases, whether Profits Hoarding or Normal Profits produced, fall off at a greatly accelerated rate due to Profits Hoarding Production during bad economic times.

The upshot of Profits Hoarding Production means it worsens bad economic conditions, dampens economic acceleration, and cuts short economic booms. Response to the Resource Market amplifies inflationary pressure, while actually consuming more resource for less Production, as it retards Capital formation in the Resource Recovery Sector. Consumer debt is always increased, sometimes double, with lessened increase in Standard of Living. Marketing dollars are always increased, with less marginal utility. Capitalization of Normal Profits Production Industries is always retarded as these industries receive less Market share of Sales and Profits. All Prices in the overall Market increase, under pressures to purchase Capital Goods from Profits Hoarding industries. Such industries and Companies extend into Normal Profits industries because of their extended Investment capacity; but show less profitability from these investments than Normal Profits Competitors. It is estimated such Profit Hoarding Companies overall triple the unemployment rate, under all economic conditions; by causing marginal profit-making Normal industries unprofitable.

Chapter IX:
The Residues of Inflation

◆

The first assertion will be quite controversial; Business and Businessmen love Inflation. This statement must be quantified: They love Inflation if it is steady, not excessive (i.e. less than 9% per year), and generated evenly throughout the Economy. The rationale is easy; Business enjoys the natural aggregation of their Capital, the ability to increase their prices, the decreasing cost of their debt load, and the higher numeral profits coming from the higher pricing. They have the ability to suppress their own operating costs, by resisting Wage increases to their own employees, and delaying payment for raw materials. They glow in Investor confidence over higher Sales volumes in Dollar terms, with higher dividend returns in Dollars. They enjoy easy ability to increase their own salaries and benefits faster than the Inflation rate. Lastly, Businessmen face slowed Capital Growth rates with slower Construction due to pricing; so they find themselves with less to manage at higher pay.

Deflation possesses all the opposite effects for the Business leader, so He curses flat pricing schedules. His workload increases, the margins of profitability are lessened, Wage demands of employees remain relatively constant because of Seniority demands, Investor confidence is not bolstered by constancy of Profit levels, and He cannot ask for exorbitant salaries and benefit increases. Actual deflation holds absolute Nightmares for the Businessman. Raw materials always increase as a percentage of operating costs, Employees are gaining in Wage value without ability on his part to reduce said value without losing skilled labor assets, profit margins are shrinking in Production, and Investors lose confidence at shrinking Profits while mumbling of salary and benefit reductions to reflect their own dividend reductions.

The astute Businessman quickly notes an essential characteristic of economic life; an Inflationary economy widens the pay gap between himself and his employees. A Price stable, or deflationary economy, narrows the gap in income between himself and his employees. The Businessman comes to the belief that good economic times requires some level of Inflation, else the economy is in bad shape. This leads the Businessmen to devise pricing schedules which are inflationary, and resist adamantly any reductions from the schedules devised. These Businessmen will even quadruple Marketing budgets to get Product sold, without lowering price schedules to increase Consumer Demand; increased Marketing budgets being an easy sell to Stockholders. This tendency of Businessmen provides Ninety percent of the resistance to deflationary pressures.

The modern Economy is not a free market system. The current Republican administration demanded a Tax Cut, rather than paying off some proportion of the National Debt. They did so because Republicans feared disturbance to the financial market, not from fear the Democrats would spend the Money on welfare programs. The release of such largesse of funds would have changed the matrix of Market Entrants into competition, lowering Price schedules in the long-run. Such funds would have been directed to precisely those Industries showing the highest profitability (i.e. Profits Hoarding, relative Black Market pricing industries). The estimated increased competition was very unwelcome to Corporate leadership, who were heavy Republican political contributors. The were unopposed by National Debt holders who would have had interrupted interest payments on their Notes, and would have to find other profitable alternatives for investment. Elimination of Debt, when it would increase competition, is not a priority.

Adamant resistance to Deflation can be found in Business leadership, Real Estate Agencies, and Property holders. Real Estate Agents receive commissions on the total value of Sale; they consistently turn down offers for purchase which are not at least a four percent increase over the previous purchase for the Property in question. They often do so without informing the Property holder, who may have been waiting years to sell the Property. Property holders often find Real Estate Agencies opposed to any reductions in sell price; and Property holders may find sell contracts give Agents a lengthy duration to sell the Property—up to two years. The resistance of Business leadership to deflationary pressure has already been noted. Property holders often expect financial reward for simple possession of Property. A glaring example is a Homeowner known to the Author: The Homeowner purchased the House for Thirty Thousand Dollars some Thirty years previously; living in the House for approximately $10,000 per year. He gleefully accepted the Realtor's suggestion He add $10,000 for each year He had lived in the residence. The Real Estate Agent assured him of a Sale. The Homeowner sold the House four years later, doing so personally to get it sold, and accepted a price of $125,000. The Homeowner commented later he did not understand why the Fifty year old House did not sell. The Author comments it had been initially built for $12,000.

The above illustrates a tendency of elements in the Economy to depend on a certain rate of Inflation as a source of income. There are innumerable impediments to deflationary pressures, which range from set tax rates to Government assistance payments. A example is a Property holder who had to tear down a 125 year old shed on a lot, to get his property assessment reduced from $4700 per year, to a more equitable $700. A COLA decrease in Social Security benefits would have

Senior Citizens rioting in the Streets. Tobacco is a case where Government continues to raise an excise tax, to maintain a price on a product. It is unknown to most Consumers, but the Government does the same with Gasoline. Liquor and Coffee also join this splendid list. Less excitable products are Tires and Phone products. The Government has increased the excise taxes throughout the Economy for the last Thirty years, to where such taxes provide more income than does the Capital Gains Tax plus the Corporate Income Tax. A important aspect of keeping such taxes hidden from Consumers, lay in maintaining Product pricing. The Government, itself, goes to tremendous efforts to forestall deflationary pressures.

Banks and Individuals on set incomes contain the great core of opponents of Inflation, simply because They are the economic element most injured by it. Governmental workers actually prefer some level of Inflation; it allowing for advanced Government supplement to pension and medical plans, which tend to stay ahead of the Curve. Workers are split on the issue of Inflation; blue collar workers being behind the curve in Wage scales, while white collar and professional trades in favor of it due to their ability to stay ahead of the curve through setting their own salaries and charges. All of the above cited are to some degree wrong.

Banks acquire the highest percentage of deposits during period of Inflation. Individuals on set incomes rely on Government subsistence, traditionally generating higher standards of living than set incomes alone, in times of no Inflation. Governmental Civil Service find Private Sector equal positions acquiring higher pay faster than Government service; this to make up for insecurity of pension and medical plans. Inflation impels blue collar labor to seek other employment, invariably better-paid than previous employment. White collar and professional Trades face Profitability ceilings from which to draw pay; subject to rising material and Products cost. Business leaders find it impossible to retire or sell out; their incomes immediately start to degrade.

Government loses possibly most of all, as expenditures increase while tax rates do not inflate. Government must resort to deficit spending, unless real tax rates can match the increases in Inflation; rarely attainable with Government being the largest Purchaser in the Economy.

A second essential characteristic of Inflation must now be examined. Inflation inserts a split between Capital and Profitability, to the exact degree of Inflation. This rationale is much easier explained than understood. Economic Capital increases in value with a given rate of Inflation. Holding on to Capital in inflationary times brings an increase in the sale price of the property on the Market. Profitability on the Capital, though, must increase by a like rate; otherwise there is devaluation on the actual Productive value. This Profitability must increase to difference between the old rate of Production and the new rate of Production after Inflation, plus the inflationary rate exacted on the Profits, to maintain real quotient profitability value. Lack of maintenance causes Capital cost increments above the current rate of Inflation, while the real productivity quotient falls. This model has many pitfalls.

Economics states simply lower real production quotients leads to higher costs of production, and longer amortization rates with higher Capital Cost for item produced. Remember the real production quotients have no relationship to actual production levels; they register only the intermix of material, Capital equipment, and labor to produce Product. Old Ranchers used to talk about being Range-poor or Cattle-poor. Homeowners Today will mention living in expensive homes with higher tax assessments, higher mortgage payments, and longer Mortgages. The longer Mortgages are achieved with refinancing already owned structures. Homeowners find their costs of living increasing faster than the inflation rate and Household income.

Business suffers from an even worse situation; they must achieve the increased Profits in the face of limited product price expansion without loss of Sales volume. These businesses have static costs: Plant, property taxes, fuel, electricity, Mortgage payments, distribution and Marketing costs, warehousing costs, and materials purchase; all of which are outside their ability to reduce. Business has little control over anything other than Labor; who finds rising Layoffs, lower revised Wage schedules, and more unpaid leave. Business maintains its profits at the cost of destabilizing the living standard of their Labor force.

We have now arrived at the essential argument of this Chapter; Inflation invariably brings instability to the Economy. It acts as an inhibiting nemesis to Production, providing higher material and operating costs. It increases Labor instability; Production falls through loss of skilled labor, and Workers face losses of income. It becomes increasingly difficult to sustain profitability of production, without increases of Sales volume; impossible with decreasing Production, and price inelasticity of Product. Recapitalization schedules will be scaled down, with correspondent losses of Production. Businessmen think of Downsizing, a stopgap to attain Profitability; worsening later Profits forecasts due to loss of experience. Business throughout the late 1980s and early 1990s sought to Out-Source their Production; a fright of lost quality and Head Office attempt to replace Production, and still keep Production Profitability. The effect of Inflation remains the second Evil, right behind Recession.

Examination of the effects of Inflation can make One shudder at the disruption to the Economy. Every round of Inflation studied produces one observation initially; root cause remains Business attempt to increase Profit share of Production. Corporate Price schedules persist in maintaining a steady Price increase for their Products, even though their Production costs decrease through technological advance. An Economic description would be refusal to pass on Production savings to the Consumer. The Consumer is expected to capitalize the cost of new technology, but not share in the Profitability of the technology. Business, by this practice, demands the Consumer fund the increased efficiency without reward.

Consumers left with the old Price schedules, Business re-enter into the Pricing Market with higher funding; driving up the Price of all elements. Consumers, in their capacity as Labor, demand higher Wages to compete for the same Product mix previously enjoyed. Employers are forced to give Wage increases over the long run, and initial Pricing scalpers raise their own Prices to keep the Profits they desire. Consumers insist on higher Wages, and the Cycle repeats. This debacle drives the Inflationary cycle, until Those on set incomes must desist from purchase of Products. The Inflationary cycles persist for extenuated Periods, because of Government transfer payments to the Poor. It devolves to the Point where blue collar Labor turns into working Poor, and cannot purchase; therefore Production drops into Recession due to lack of Sales.

Blue Collar Labor works as hard, if not as well, as any segment of the Labor force. They do not deserve to be dropped into the category of Poor, simply because Corporate management desires economic profits. Economic profits are very distinct from entrepreneurial profits. Economists term profits to be economic when such Profits are derived outside the normal Production Costs structure. The Market inability to force Corporate management to pass Production Costs savings on to the Consumers in lower prices; puts such Profits clearly inside the Realm of economic profits. What does this mean to the Pricing Schedule?

Economic profits can best be thought to be Profits which are undeserved, because they are based on factors other than Production Costs. Normal entrepreneurial profits are an inherent element in Normal Production Costs Schedules. Economic Profits are Profits over and above normal entrepreneurial profits, achieved by some Market share or shortage. Study of this Work were acquaint One with the fact this is the same definition of a Black Market. Corporate management who refuse to pass on savings in the costs of Production, are engaged in

Black Marketing; a definition which would shock most of the Participants in such Corporate practice.

Tax Policy stands as the only vehicle to combat such Black Marketing. Government possesses the only Power effective enough to limit such excesses. The problem here lies in the fact Corporate management stands as the largest contributors to Political campaigns. They in fact provide some Ninety percent of the Soft Money contributions made; either through Corporate leadership, funded Political Action Committees, or direct Corporate grants to Political Parties. The funds come from Black Market pricing as seen. Current Politicians operate in the present system, and do not know how to raise such funding by other means. Real truth would admit this funding could not be found elsewhere. American Voters would finds their elected officials abandoning the expensive airways, in their attempts to gain reelection. It remains doubtful Tax Policy will be initiated to stop this practice.

The sole Curative for the current Black Market pricing, without Government intervention, remains a sad one. A shrinking Labor pool will insist on higher pay for Labor, especially in a milieu of ageing population. The trouble with this solution will be it requires years, and has an adverse counter-veiling force. Politicians funded by Black Marketeers will insure substantial levels of youthful immigrants to fill Labor rolls. The shrinking Labor pool will still apply, because of the ageing of the World population; but it may mean a American population of one-half billion people for the United States. Our major cities may resemble Calcutta, Cairo, and New Delhi before Corporation have to surrender Black Market profits.

The current round of Terrorism expresses the dangers of Over-Population. The Terrorism evolves as Territorial demands effected by people who could not mount full-scale war effectively. The practice, in itself, shows the fallacy of Black Market inflationary pricing. High-tech weaponry could not be funded by the Terrorists, so they develop equally as effective high-tech weaponry to use in conjunction with natural

Capital equipment capacities; the final effect being on a par with the more expensive Military-Industrial Complex weaponry. Cheaper alternatives will eventually be devised by a Poorer educated element. The High-Tech weaponry meant Profits to the Military-Industrial Complex, Profits which were very Black Market inflationary pricing; now, those weapon systems cannot protect them, or their Profitability. Better if those weapon systems had not been built, because their residue in stored radioactive materials etc. represent base reservoirs which Terrorists could use to fashion their weapons of destruction. It is finally interesting to note the turn of Terrorist thought; they are not content with their old homelands, they wish to extend into the United States.

Chapter X: More Rational Public Policy

◆

Everyone has proposals to advance the economic performance of American society. Supply-side advocates tend to be in ascendency at the present time. The Monetarists run a close second. Supply-side insist the method of advancement consists of support of Business interests; facilitating investments through Tax credits program for Investments. Monetarists claim the method to control the Economy is manipulation of Monetary Instruments. Keynesian Economists claim Government spending fuels the Economy, with economic gain to be realized by Government expenditures. The Author will now present his own position: The above are all Crap! Normal Costs Production holds the vital key to all economic progress.

Two things affect any Economy; the first is Military Expenditures, the second is deviations from Normal Costs Production. Military Expenditures affect the Economy very seriously by production for purposes other than Consumption or future production. Military Expenditures must be considered a total waste, in Economic terms. There is no increase in the standard of living, or is there an increase in production capacity. Labor expended for War-making enterprises also imply complete waste economically. Wastage of Resource, Labor, and technology bring down-the-road decrease of Standard of Living.

Deviations from Normal Costs Production bring the second great dislocation to the Economy. The reason for this lies in the dislocation of Profits distribution. Disturbed allocation of Profits will invariably bring distortions to Consumption patterns. These distortions are always reflected in Inflation or Deflation. The real pertinency of the distortion comes from the fact Consumers of Production disappear.

Normal Costs Production contain all elements for successful production: It takes into account Resource Cost, Capital Cost, Infrastructure Cost, Labor Cost, and Entrepreneurial Profit. Taxes are accounted in Infrastructure Cost, the Two may be attributed as the same. Recapitalization is handled by Capital Cost, while Investment resides within Entrepreneurial Profits. This is the speculated ideal Economic Model, of which all Economists are so proud. They leave out Credit Cost; but It is covered by elements of Infrastructure Cost and Entrepreneurial Profits. Normal Costs Production covers all elements for successful Economic functioning for sustained Production.

The above statement holds greater truth than almost all realize! Consumption will always match Production, if Normal Costs Production progresses through the entirety of the Economy. Profits must remain undistorted; Normal Costs Production model of distribution of Profits must be in force. Problems of Over-Supply, also known as Under-Consumption, will not occurs where the Profits are distributed to the correct Sectors. Over-Capitalization, otherwise known as Under-Utilization of Capital Equipment, will not occur with Normal Costs Production distribution of Profits. There will literally be no Inflation or Deflation (functionally untrue due to Credit extension, as noted above. Credit extension means younger people living above their means; but is not important to the Analysis as it is a standard programable factor.)

The above structure says quietly, and therefore unheard, no Fuel is necessary for the Economy in the first place. Normal Costs Production will generate Sales, provide for it's own recapitalization, propel new

Investment, and support full employment. Welfare transfer payments are covered by Infrastructure Costs, and decrease to zero as distribution of Profits is equalized. Credit Extension exhibits an Inflation, but only in the Resource Market; lowering the Standard of Living only by a standard 2.3% overall. This decrease must be seen as much more viable, than an ordinary unemployment rate of Eight percent. The Credit extension does not affect Normal Costs Production otherwise; and benefits by reduction of Welfare transfer payments.

Economists exist who say Taxes are a detriment, which must be corrected by providing propellent for Investment. This is patently untrue! Infrastructure Costs must be factored into Normal Costs Production; though it is true Taxes can exceed Normal Costs structuring, and cause distortion of the distribution of Profits. Government can engage in Black Market inflationary pricing, as well as the Private Sector. Most models the Author has worked suggest Infrastructure Costs should not exceed Twelve percent of the total Cost of Production. Excesses of the derived figure calls for Governmental downsizing! So-called Propellants do not deal with the problem of downsizing, while shifting the Tax impact shifts the distribution of Production Profits as Labor elements are over-taxed.

Monetarists claim regulation of Financial Instruments generate necessary liquidity for Investment. The real result is only Credit Extension, which produces a inflation based on Resource use with a predictable diminishment of the Standard of Living. Failure to provide Credit with loss of liquidity, could reduce Production levels up to Thirty percent. The area is not without heavy impact. Manipulation of Financial Instruments, though, could not effectively increase Production; except for some reduction of the diminishment in the Standard of Living, actually achievable only with excessive charges of Interest.

Clearly expressed by the above analysis comes the need for Government action to limit Profits and Products Hoarding, which leads to Inflation; the expression of distortions of Profits distribution from

Normal Costs Production allocation of Profits. Government, though, instills no confidence as a Watchdog, or Administrator. Continual pressure on Political leadership by Business leadership brings little reliability to Governmental regulation, especially when Politicians are in continual search for political campaign contributions. The only expedient may be the passage of economically effective Tax Policy; something American Voters could possibly pressure Congress and President into passage, if the Voters understood the Issue.

Correct Tax Policy remains a collection of correct Accounting procedures, mostly boredom for Everyone; but correct Analysis of Tax Policy need be made. The following will be a list of correct Accounting procedures which could be used to counteract Product and Profits Hoarding:

Standard Recapitalization Schedule of Twelve Years Duration: Business could not take depreciation loss off greater than one-twelfth of initial cost per year. Business which had to replace equipment in quicker duration can take off one-twelfth of the new equipment cost, plus one-twelfth of the old equipment cost.

Standard Amortization of Plant: Business can take off only one-twentieth of cost of said Plant per year. Shorter mortgages will have to await tax deferment.

Investment Tax Credits Limitation: Business cannot deduct an amount greater than Twelve percent of their previous year's listed Capital, as a deductible Tax Credit for Investments. More preferable is a limitation of only Tax Credit up to 75% of said Investments coupled with the above.

Limitation of Corporate Management Deduction: Limitation of deductibility of all Management salaries, bonuses, paid-up life insurance, pension plans, medical insurance, and annuities to an amount equal to Three percent of total claimed operating costs listed. The Author personally believes Corporate Management should withstand the full cost of Management, like Individual Taxpayers.

Limitation of Stock Options: Limitation of total Stock Option awards to a level equal to Two percent of outstanding Corporate stock per year. Violation of this limitation will be payment of total Corporate tax on total value of exercised stock options.

Bonus Legality: Bonuses must be distributed by percentage Sectors of Labor and Management. Bonuses to Management cannot exceed more twenty-five percent of the total Dollar awards to Labor. Bonuses awards to Management will not receive deductions if in excess. Management personnel can receive both Management and Labor awards; as recognition of the status of Management in small business.

Management Salary Limitation: Members of Management can receive Salary deductions only if such Salaries do not exceed 2000% of the lowest entry-level of the Corporation. Corporations paying Management salaries in excess of that amount cannot deduct such excess from their taxes as operating costs.

Lack of Pension Plan Surtax: Corporations which do not provide a Pension plan for Employees equal to Twenty-five percent of the Employees' Wages, must pay the projected difference as Tax from Profits greater than Eight percent of Operating Costs, if such Profits exist.

Proof of Cost Formulation: Corporations must prove operating costs which differ from the Operational norm in the Country. This is quite difficult to understand, but easy to implement. All economic functions will be catalogued by the IRS (relatively easy with Computer, if returns are properly filed by activity), then standard deviations will be taken:

Average, Mean, and Bell Curve. The highest and lowest Apertures will be studied. Those with the highest operating costs will have one year to fall within structural norms, or prove why they cannot. Failure to fall within the Standard bell will lose deduction of the excess Costs. This has two effects: It forces innovation through recapitalization, and It forces Corporations to pass Production Savings on to the Consumer. This ongoing process will continually reposition new Entrants to the Apertures; and the final product, will be proper recapitalization at the rate most economically effective.

A change of the treatment of Corporations and Business in the Courts should also be entertained. The varying size and scale of Business makes the assessment of Fines for proven liability a futile effort. A sliding scale of Fines demands Judicial personnel be trained in Economics, in order to properly assess a Fine. Large Corporate entities are never fined in the magnitude to incite aversion to further generation of Fines. Lesser Business entities are often destroyed financially by assessment of Fines. Judicial personnel, especially Tort lawyers, are quite indifferent to the impact of massive liabilities on Business interests. Laws should be changed to make all Business Fines and liabilities a percentage judgement of the Operating Costs of the Business, during the Period Year where the offense took place. The Judge or Jury should take in account in decision of the percentage to be assessed; how many were injured by the offense, how much of the operational structure of the Business was involved in the offense, how much of the offense was due to the operational negligence of what percentage of the Operational staff, and finally, the exact largesse of the expected assignment of liability. Judges to automatically revise the size of the assignment of liability to match guidelines set up by either the U.S. Supreme Court, or the United States Justice Department.

Implicit in the proposed change is the understanding there are differing levels in ability to pay. Also inherent in this endeavor comes the knowledge some degree of Accident and offense will occur in production activities, no matter how great the caution. The liability must be shared to some degree; the rationale for Governmental medical services in the first place. No Agent, whether Offender, or Injured, should derive windfall wealth, or destructive loss from normal Accidents. Criminal dereliction leading to vast injuries should be treated as Physical Assault cases, with Prison penalties assigned to guilty Parties.

The influence of Monetarists should be restrained, though Financial Instruments are very important to Credit Extension. Interest rates should always remain high, to combat Inflation. The minimum for Business loans should be at Seven percent, the minimum for Consumer loans should be Fourteen percent, and Mortgage rates should never fall below Six percent. The above floors may seem harsh, but they are sufficiently low as not to inhibit Production. Their magnitude reverses the inflationary pressure of the Credit Extension; Borrowers lose the expansion of their purchasing power, by curtailment of their discretionary spending; while they can still live above their means. The high percentage on Business loans limits the number of Entrants into the Production process, allowing existing business to sell it's production at Normal Costs operation. The high rate of Mortgage extension demands purchase within the Buyer's ability to sustain; meaning they opt for housing within their budgetary incomes to maintain.

Curtailment of Government spending, which can sharply alter the distribution of Production Profits, has been a Gordian knot. Everyone has their own formula to reduce Government spending; none of the formula work, whether coming from Economist, Politician, or Man in the Street. A current Surplus was destroyed by Tax cuts, even though Federal Debt remains high. A probable solution could be passage of Federal Law stipulating the IRS service the Federal Debt with a One percent per year repayment schedule, before They are allowed to place Funds in the general Treasury. The previous could be further broken into Quarters, for maintenance of payments for Government obligations. This Plan has no benefit, except for insistence Federal legislators publicly announce desire for deficit spending; entailing Public debate of deficit spending for proposed Projects.

A second initiative could be a mandated legislative review of all Labor levels of Federal Agencies, Bureaus, departments, and environs. Each head of department, at every level, must prove his need for every employee in Committee hearing; the largesse of such endeavor would require each Senator and Legislator would have to individually hear Cases for about Two weeks of the year. The legislator would write his findings, and would advance them at full Committee hearing of Ten or More–such Committee probably being mixed with Senators and Congressmen. Budget allowance would be made only for necessary Labor components; it would be up to the Department Head to schedule Works loads where all Employees shared the required hours until Labor rolls were reduced. All Civil Service Pensions and benefits would have to be changed to reflect actual number of hours worked by each Employee.

A combined Committee jointly chaired by Senators and Congressmen should be created, for the simple purpose of reporting to Congress as a Whole, which Weaponry systems of the Military should be scraped. Their sole task would be to investigate the research and development records of each Weapon system, to see whether design and performance goals were being maintained. Military expenditure remains an economic waste; but We can insist on Bang for the Buck. Failures to maintain original Goals must be reported to Congress, along with the exact nature of the failure of the Systems, and recommended action taken. The Process would hopefully kill two dozen sick Proposals, where already in-place weapon systems show higher per-formance and viability. The fact the Committee would have to report to the Congress and enter into the Public Record; could bring greater hon-esty with less surrender to Special Interests.

A simple way to control Political 'Soft Money' contributions could be to pass legislation which places a Twelve percent tax on all such grants, if made by other than individual American Citizens qualified to vote. This would not eliminate such contributions, but would not allow Corporate structures to buy political influence through evasion of legitimate taxes. It would also penalize foreign Contributors who sought to buy influence. Added benefit comes in the form Felons also have to pay such tax, reducing the influence of Individuals already convicted of White Collar crimes; they are not able to Vote until all Probations and Paroles are up. The final advantage comes from the fact it will be a source of revenue, not directly associated with taxation of American taxpayers.

The problem of Corporate Sector Accounting remains as a Profits Hoarding problem, with no easy solution. A positive partial solution could be insistence Corporations who claim to loan funds to Sectors and Consumer Credit be ordered to file as financial institutions, in order to claim these deductions. Their charter as financial institutions clears the way to demand payment into the Federal Deposit Insurances Corporations for all funds claimed. This practice will further guarantee Individual Depositors' funds with a extended source of revenue. Later Corporate claims against the FDIC can be forestalled by requiring proof the entire Corporation showed loss, while payment would be only of the percentage of Sector credit loss. This may seem like trickery, but Sector accounting itself resides only on trickery.

A further elimination of Profits Hoarding can be achieved and protection of Workers can be effected; by giving legal status to Pension plans and Benefits. The Law would simply state Retirement plans, Medical Plans, Profit-sharing plans hold the de facto status of Contract. This legality would dictate Corporations had to stand responsible for their obligations to Workers. Corporations could not sell off Sectors, to absolve financial commitments made to Employees. The Corporation would have to negotiate and sell financial obligations to Employees at the time of the Sector sale; or retain financial responsibility for those obligations. The practice of raffling off Sector plants to absolve obligations to Employees would end. Employees who labored under promise of future benefits could not be dismissed, by transfer of Title. The practice of borrowing against Pension plans, or reinvestment of such Pension funds in the Corporation operations, could also be legislatively restrained; by insistence of a outside Financial Institution of Trust being named who would hold such deposits, and approve such Investment of Pension funds only under Federal Banking structure rules.

The California Energy Crisis outlines another glaring fact; the need to regulate the dispersal of Dividends. California Energy Producers deliberately reduced the Recapitalization Schedules after Deregulation; fully expecting to initiate an Energy Crisis, but buying support from Stockholders by payment of excessive Dividends. These Energy Producers expected a huge increase in their charges to Consumers, so They could recapitalize quickly in Crisis. Corporate Management was criminally responsible for the Energy Crisis, though they bought a closed settlement.

A Federal Dividend Fund need to be established to forestall such practice. Each Corporation would be required to deposit Ten percent of their yearly Dividend into the Fund, for a period of either Three or Five years. The Fund would be mandated with repayment of overcharges to Consumers, by Management malfeasance. Fund investigators would be charged with receiving complaints from Consumers, investigating such complaints, and deciding whether to prosecute in Federal Court of suspected Violators. Only a Court decision would release such Funds to Consumers as rebates. The Court would decide whether the Violator was Innocent, guilty of Incompetence, or guilt of Criminal negligence; at which time proper fines or punishment would be assessed. The rebates to Consumers would be assessed equally against all Corporate accounts; insuring Corporate anger against such practice. The salaries of all Employees of the Fund are to be drawn equally from all Corporate accounts; but are mandated not to exceed Two percent of the received Dividends per year. The Federal Dividend Fund is also to operate from a set budget.

The operation of Federal Safety Regulatory agencies should also be changed, to speed the pace of enforcement. These Agencies are to be limited in Employment to Directors, Policy Board and Staff, and Investigators. Such Agencies are to be legally restrained from demands for written records of compliance. Investigators will be given legal right to assess Fines, from $500 to $10,000 per individual instance; or per day, until the hazard is cleaned up. These Fines must be immediately paid by Violator; else Investigator will exercise his power to notify local, State, or Federal law enforcement to shut down Plant operations. Said Violator can appeal to a Federal Court for redress, if he believes the Fines to be excessive; where the Safety Agencies must appear with legal counsel. The Federal Law changing the mode of Safety regulation should dictate Eighty percent of the operating budget of such Agencies go to pay field Investigators. Business has the burden of paperwork lifted from their shoulders, Federal Agencies are limited in deadweight staff, and Spot inspections will lead Business to comply with the Safety regulations outlined by the Policy staff, rather than falsify paperwork which is never checked.

This Country has the poorest compliance rate among all industrialized nations, in meeting mandated environmental standards. Soft Money have incited Congress after Congress to relax set standards for Pollution control, while Courts relax EPA fines and ability to police industries. Law should be implemented which limits the right to privacy to Individuals, with law enforcement agents legally allowed anywhere Employees have access. Records are treated in the same way; Employee access allows for law enforcement access. EPA fines are also to be dismissed as a venue to punish non-compliant Business. Law will entail EPA officials through Consideration Committee of at least Three Individuals will assess limitation of Dividend and Bonus programs for said Business; at rates of segments of 5% up to 80% of total payments of Dividends and Bonuses, said funds to be used solely for environmental protection systems. Corporate Management or Stockholders can appeal such assessments in Federal Courts.

Many will say the above proposals remind of a Fireman chasing a fire with a bucket of water. The reality consists of a wholly different median. Democracies never move rapidly, in definition of their operational constraints. Changing the Status Que requires altering the Mind set of the majority of the Populace. Incremental steps can survive the discussion process, most grand plans cannot. Small improvements allow for consistency, and in this case; a gradual reduction of Corporate Profits.

Chapter XI: Discussion of Inflation on Lifestyle

◆

We viewed previously Inflation was only reflection of distortions of distribution of Profits. An analysis proving such assertion was not advanced at that time; and so must enter here. The Author will not bore with a group of Economic equations, which he might erroneously construct anyway. Know simply raw materials and manufactured goods increase in Price if more Individuals bid for them; a limited supply goes to those who bid most. It is what is called the blind hand of the Market. Economists tell Us Market forces ideally handle any pricing situation. This could be true at a base level of technological production; but it is even doubtful there. Technology brings Economics of Specialization; Goods being produced of different complexity and difficulty of production. Economists explain the simpler forms of differentiation between Goods, using such terms as Complementary Good, Competitive Goods, Resource-Conflictive Goods, Heavy-Capitalization Goods, Elastic Goods, and Inelastic Goods.

These terms specify the methods by which Product or Profits Hoarding can be introduced to interfere with the blind hand of the Market. Gasoline is a complimentary good to Automobiles; One will accept even $10 per gallon of Gasoline, if he has spent $100,000 plus on a BMW. Oil Producers know this fact, and tend to raise their price for

Gasoline; even when there is more than adequate supply of Gasoline. Economic terms state Complementary Goods enjoy an environment subject to economic profits; this simply means Complementary Goods producers can charge higher than Normal Costs Production pricing. Individuals with heavy Investment in a Complementary Good increase their need of supportive goods. The economic profits for the Complementary Goods suppress the buying potential of Consumers, leading them to demand higher return for their own labor; this termed inflationary pressure. Inflation is the dollar increase of their success in doing so.

Competitive Goods can also enjoy an environment subject to economic profits. Knowledge of limitation of production Market fulfillment by Competitive Goods producers, leads all producers to raise Prices above Normal Costs Production pricing; they cannot lose their share of the Market. This excites the same inflationary pressures among Consumers, with reciprocal Inflation. The blind hand of the Market fails again.

Resource-Conflictive Goods may also allow for economic profits; Producers with knowledge Consumer Demand for Conflictive Goods not of such magnitude to drain Resources markedly. These Producers often use statements of Resource Market high pricing, to institute above Normal Costs Production pricing. The results are the same!

Heavy-capitalization Goods recognize there is extreme demand for their Product, and realize competition for their Market share will not arise quickly. The largesse of Investment, and time of Plant construction, limits quantity and speed of Entrants into the Market. They introduce above Normal Costs Production pricing. It duly creates inflationary pressure as Consumers of their Product try to equalize their Purchase structure.

Elastic and Inelastic Goods refer to the degree Product Price affects the Consumption levels of a Good. Elastic Goods possess a wide swing of Consumption levels, dictated by Price of the Good. Inelastic Goods have a more constant Consumer Demand, no matter what the Price level is. Elastic Goods do not enjoy an environment viable for economic profits. Inelastic Goods possess the perfect environment to generate economic profits. A converse explanation comes with the statement: Elastic Goods Producers suffer from Inflation; Inelastic Goods Producer can pass inflationary costs to the Consumer.

Referral was made earlier of Profits Hoarding segments of the Economy, who could profit from the ability to increase Prices over Normal Costs Production pricing; while the rest of the Economy could not. Inelastic Goods engage in Profits Hoarding, and Elastic Goods Production face reductions in Consumer Demand and Production. What does it all mean to the Consumer?

The most basic impact to the Consumer is increase in Prices throughout the structure, though very much not at the same rate of increase. Set Income segments of the Population are permanently injured; to most considering the average size of Set Incomes, it means being reduced to Poverty without counter-measure. The fulcrum of inflationary pressure always applies heaviest to inelastic Wage-earners; those with the least job skills and in elementary employment positions—like Custodians, Waiters and Waitresses, Gas Station Attendants, and Store Clerks. They have only Ten percent of the Power to demand Wage increases, as do Collegiate level positions. Their life subsistence demands They expend at least 37% of the income spent by Collegiate level position holders. Inelastic Wage job-holders face absolute inability to Save; their only hope for later life is Social Security and Employer's pension plans. Less than 14% of these positions are covered by adequate pension plans.

Specialized Trades and Plant Workers split into who work for Profits Hoarding enterprise, and those who do not. The Workers of Profits Hoarding companies generally express a rising standard of living, as Employers pay for good Labor Relations. Specialized Trades and Plant Workers who work for Inelastic Goods industries which do not Profit Hoard, find themselves with a falling standard of living. Specialized

Trades and Plant Workers working for Elastic Goods industries which are not Profit Hoarding industries most generally maintain their standard of living, though lack seriously the same retirement and medical benefits as their contemporaries in Profits Hoarding industries or Normal Costs production Inelastic Goods industries..

Government workers split in two levels: Trades and Collegiate level positions. The Trade level Civil Service find themselves with falling standard of living, though generally their retirement plans are on a par with Profits Hoarding company Employees. Collegiate level Civil Service Employees find Entry-level salaries keeping pace with Profits Hoarding enterprise; but face much-reduced pay increases thereafter, often having to apply for higher positions in Civil Service to maintain their standard of living. They cannot keep pace with their Profits Hoarding companies Employee-contemporaries; though they run equivalent to Co-workers in the Inelastic Goods industries with Normal Costs Production..

Study of the origins of Millionaires in this Country find almost all come from Inelastic Goods Industries; Ninety percent from Profits Hoarding Enterprise. Further examination expresses almost all Capital formation for Elastic Goods industries come from Inelastic Goods industries; but here is a vital rub, Profits Hoarding Enterprise Capital provides only about Thirty percent of Elastic Goods industries Capitalization. Profits hoarding Entrepreneurial Capital shows far greater likelihood to fund Inelastic Goods industries, which they turn into Profits Hoarding enterprise. Studies indicate the Elastic Goods Sectors to be as much as Forty percent underfunded.

A most disquieting development comes in the fact some of the most Elastic Goods Sectors are completely dependent on Profits Hoarding industries. A prime example comes from Agriculture, which is dependent on farm equipment, fuel, irrigation equipment, fertilizer and Seed. All of these industries express high propensity for Profits Hoarding. Agriculture has not been able to support itself since the 1920s. Retail

Sales begins to show all the disabilities as had Agriculture, with rising bankruptcies, over-priced showroom space, escalating electrical bills, and immense property tax assessments. Margins of profitability are decreasing, and overall Wage rates are dropping in the industry. The Liquor industry shows evidence of pricing itself out of the Market, while successful restaurants cater to the Rich; while Wage rates are falling with a factored inflation rate applied to Wage increases.

More and more of American industries in the Elastic Goods Sectors are closing; shipped Overseas to cheaper Producers. What essentially makes these Producers cheaper? They pay relatively the same cost for raw materials, the relative same cost for energy, the relative same cost for capital equipment; their only claim of difference in Labor cost. Why is their Labor cheaper? Labor in these foreign industries have to support extended families, because these Countries do not provide for the elderly, medical care, or retirement in most cases. There is a lower standard of living in these Nations, but the higher number of family elements supported with each Wage-earner raises the overall cost of life subsistence. This total life subsistence per Employee comes to rank with Entry-level employment in this Country. Again, Why is their Labor cheaper?

The answer to the question is simple: They hire their Employees from an Economy which runs on Normal Costs Production. The heavier population and lack of welfare transfer payments forestall development of Profits Hoarding Enterprise. Not even Credit Extension allows for such development. The lack of welfare transfer payments stops excessive monthly payments; income must go for necessities; the elasticity of Goods is far lengthened, much looser than in this Country where even the unemployed and elderly has a monthly income. Labor is much cheaper, because Goods are much cheaper; based on Normal Costs Production.

Return to Normal Costs Production in this Country would allow for recapitalization of old industries, whose Product is currently purchased

Overseas. There has been an estimated loss of Eleven Millions jobs to Overseas production since 1940. Normal Costs Production could allow for the return of almost all of these jobs. This must be qualified by stating standards of the Environmental Protection Agency would stop almost Four Million of these jobs' return. Reevaluation would state Profits Hoarding Enterprise grants ability to produce around Eight percent of the World's pollution. Return to Normal Costs Production would force Business to finally accept environmental protection as a Capital Cost. The recreation of Eleven Million jobs in this County brings an Eighteen percent increase in the Standard of Living; when considering the spread Tax base, elimination of welfare transfer payments, and an estimated overall drop of Prices by Ten percent, at the minimum.

A major problem of Product and Profits Hoarding comes in the provision of Product. Product Hoarding causes huge Price increases, and avarice leads to provision of inferior product; the old analogy of a wind-broke horse. Any facsimile will do, and hurried production for sale brings loss of quality control. Profits Hoarding has even greater impact on quality of Product. Profits Hoarding insists on windfall Profits, windfall Growth rates, and windfall Capital accumulation of all Participants. High Sales volume at the inflated Prices becomes a must.

High Sales volume with Profits Hoarding holds great difficulty. Huge marketing efforts have to be made, instilling Consumer desire; no great loss to Corporations, which turn Marketing into it's own Sector with projected Profit levels. The Consumer is convinced they need the Products offered. Corporations learn to provide their own Consumer Credit, which actually raises the price of the Product some Thirty-Forty percent; not a great cost to Corporations in Sector management, with it's own projected Profits. An intelligent Corporation then analyzes the situation; there is insufficient Consumers to maintain the Sales volume, if the Product is of too high a quality.

The answer to the quandary quickly develops, shortened Life expectancy. Profits Hoarding Enterprise finds engineered obsolescence raises Sales volume, without adversely affecting Marketing efforts; already high to counteract impact of high Prices. Consumer awareness must be avoided; therefore, Product Parts are tripled in Price while Maintenance Service is turned into it's own Sector, with it's own Profit levels. The Consumer is convinced it is cheaper to buy new, than to Service. Marketing has again paid for itself; there is a huge Market for used Product, where Consumer must insist on a trade-in. Warranty program to mollify Consumers; luckily, Warranty programs can be turned into their own Sector, with their own Profit levels. Warranties determined for projected lack of exercise; extensions are offered at high pricing for profitability to the Warranty Program Sector. Corporations make their Profits whether Consumers purchase their Warranties or not; through new Sales, Maintenance profits, or Warranties profits. This Author, plus many Engineers, estimate there should be Cars on the Road, which could travel a half Million miles with only $2000 of Maintenance, and only 15% of Interior wear of Today; there are not.

The provision of other Profits Hoarding Enterprise products follow similar course. Almost half of the current Computer turnover come from planned obsolescence; this achieved by writing software of greater utility, which will not operate on older models. Programs for use on older Computer models can, and have been written; Patent rights purchased by Computer Hardware and Software Giants. A Mean Computer should have a life expectancy of Seven to Nine years; the turnover rate is Three to Four years–depending upon model. The discussion does not even have to be entered; concerning Coffee makers, radios, TVs, watches, Eyeglasses, refrigerators, Cameras, Fans, Air Conditioners, Light bulbs, Shoes, kitchen equipment, and sporting goods. Many other Goods could be added to the list; all Profits Hoarding Enterprise supplied.

This highlights the major cost to the Consumer of Profits Hoarding; the Consumers buy such products on average some Thirty percent sooner than he should have to do, and has to pay approximately forty percent more for these Products than he should have to do. One would think it not too horrible of a price to pay, for his Standard of Living. He would be wrong. The Average Consumer in American society pays 35-40% of his discretionary income per year for products produced by Profits Hoarding Enterprise. A Consumer making $20,000 per year can pay up to $3200 per year in Profits to Profits Hoarders; Normal Costs Production would entail payment of only $960 per year. What could such an Individual do with an additional $2240?

Reality states Profits Hoarding absorbs almost all the Savings ratio of ordinary American workers Today. Saving of Ten percent of yearly income per year for Forty years, when that Income is compounded every Ten years, will allow for Capital accumulation of over Ten times an Individual's salary. Only a few would be financially conscientious to properly invest their excess savings; but many would save half of the Income saved. The Profits accruing to Profits Hoarding Enterprise could stabilize the lifestyles of American Workers, rather than giving windfall gains to Corporate management.

THE REAL COSTS PRODUCTION MODEL

◆

Economic models abound as every Economic study uses it's own array of data. Each model differs to some degree, because of the exact relationships examined and evaluated. Two studies using the same model often come up with variances, because of the statistical alignment of computation. Exact replication of results can be impossible, even utilizing the same model and progression of computation, due to degree of accuracy detailed. Many are put off by the inconsistencies. They should not be, for Economic modeling is the study of Parameters. These boundaries expand and contract, yet contain the same relevance in a contained locale; much like working with Set theory in Algebra. The Intersections remain the same, only more or less defined.

The Real Costs Production Model includes all the Costs of Production–Land, Labor, Plant, Capital Equipment, Taxes, Material Costs, Transport Costs, Recapitalization, Marketing, and Entrepreneurial Profits. Some Economic Theorists, including the Author, believe the Ideal Real Costs Production Model is a balanced Model, where every one of these Costs of Production possess a perfect relationship with every other Cost. This harmony within the Ideal model forestalls any need for Economic tampering; no need for stimulus, fuel, excessive marketing efforts, or financial instrument manipulation.

Production provides for it's own regeneration through Capital accumulation. Consumer Demand is maintained through adequate Wages, to establish sufficient discretionary income. Taxes are so restrained as to not inhibit Investment, or Consumer discretionary income. The Ideal model of Real Costs Production will not degenerate into Recession; while a consistent and steady rate of Growth continues ad infinitum.

Every honest Economist should admit the Ideal model of Real Costs Production has never been in existence; and never will be. The rationale for it's preclusion lies in the need for provision of Credit to Consumers. The provision of Credit allows Consumers to live above their means; an estimated increase in the Standard of Living of a normal Twenty-three percent. The failure to provide Credit would lead to lessened production schedules, less profitability for Production, and a minimum unemployment rate of better than Eight percent. This extension of Credit exacts a predictable Inflation rate of a centered 1.3 percent annually. This Inflation rate exacted from higher Resource Costs and added Interest payments.

The extension of Credit for consumption has little other effect on the Real Costs Production model, other than the set 1.3% annual Inflation. Normal Profits of Production on the added Product pays for all the associated Costs of Production, plus the added Resource Cost and Interest. A correct balance between the other Costs of Production preclude any need to tamper with Model; no stimulus packages or extended Marketing efforts. Production should continue to prosper with the proper balance.

A examination of normal balance of Costs of Production should be the first priority. This Author has examined many Economic models, and has come up with his own conclusions. His primary conclusion consists of the belief that normal entrepreneurial Profits should not exceed One percent of Volume of Production per month, or Twelve percent annual Profit. The Reader must understand this is a general overall average; due to the specific criteria for Production for each Industry, this annual Profit could vary from 8-14% depending on specific economic activity. He also finds Taxation should never exceed the Normal Profits of the Industry; Taxation including Property taxes, Corporate taxes, and Utilities use taxes. This limitation on Taxation should not include Unemployment Fund, Social Security, and mandated Profit-sharing plans; all of these elements must be construed at Labor Costs.

Rent (cost of Land), Capital amortization, and Recapitalization schedules cannot total more than Twenty-five percent of the total Costs of Production; else Production faces potential loss of Consumer Demand. Utilities Cost, Marketing Cost, and Transport Cost should never exceed Ten percent of total Costs of Production; lest they face over-capitalization through interaction of Recapitalization schedules. The rest of total Costs of Production should be spread between Material Costs, and benefits to Labor.

Material Costs face over-capitalization; whenever they present a matrix higher than Twenty percent of total Costs of Production. The profitability of their Capitalization will fall rapidly, with extended provision of resource. Optimum Profitability in the Resource Recovery industry rests on round-the-Clock use of Capital equipment, with a Fifty hour Week for Employees (Overtime being cheaper than Capitalization, in both the Short and Long Run). Labor need get all the residual benefit of Production in the Real Costs Production model, simply to maintain the discretionary income necessary for Peak Consumer Demand; remember, extension of Consumer Credit demands repayment plus Service Charges and Interest. This demands Consumer viability, and stability of Living Standard. Anything other than sustained Consumer Demand will lead to curtailment of Production, otherwise known as Recession.

Lawrance George Lux